"This beautiful narrative from the center of our e? intimate and authentic bɪₒᵣₐₚₕy wɪth nature, magic and history. Able to transcend a self-absorbed story solely of personal transformation, Jaya's own transformative growth journey is honored by her chronicling of Don Agustin Rivas' life story and his path to knowledge. In the spirit of biographies of other great spiritual leaders and teachers, Amazon Magic brings to English, the life of a man, a culture and a territory — the Amazon. The book reflects both the rapaciousness of American and colonial practices and the resilience and renewing strength of spirit of the people and land who remain. In the reading, we are left with a sense of responsibility, humility and wonder."

> — WINONA LADUKE, internationally acclaimed activist, Green Party vice-presidential candidate in 1996, and author of *Last Standing Woman.*

"This new biography of the well-known Peruvian mestizo *ayahuasquero* Don Agustin Rivas Vasquez relates unexpunged accounts of his precocious and enterprising childhood growing up in the raw frontier towns of Amazonia during the 1940s and 1950s, and it presents candid anecdotal tales of his later explorations into the eclectic healing world of mestizo *ayahuasca* shamanism. By preserving the distinctive flavor and folkstyle of Don Agustin's unabashed narratives, Jaya Bear has created an ethnographic document that reveals an insider's view of the fantastic world of Amazonian shamanism."

> — TIMOTHY WHITE, editor of *Shaman's Drum* magazine.

"A fascinating and motivating biography! Jaya Bear portrays the spirit world of nature, through the warmth and knowledge of Don Rivas, close to a reality we can all understand."

> — BRANT SECUNDA, Huichol shaman and director of the Dance of the Deer Foundation Center for Shamanic Studies.

"Amazon Magic is a fascinating and compelling account of a shamanic tradition and a way of life disappearing as quickly as the rain forests that shaped it. Don Agustin is a complex, charismatic character who will remind readers of the teachers of Castenada. It is a 'must read' for those interested in indigenous cultures."

> — WABUN WIND, co-author, *The Medicine Wheel: Earth Astrology* and author of *Woman of the Dawn* and *Lightseeds.*

AMAZON MAGIC

The Life Story of
Auyahuasquero and Shaman
Don Agustin Rivas Vasquez

Jaya Bear

Colibri Publishing
Taos, New Mexico

Published by
Colibri Publishing
PO Box 1950
El Prado, New Mexico 87529

Library of Congress Cataloging-in-Publication Data

Bear, Jaya.
    Amazon magic : the life story of ayahuasquero
and shaman Don Agustin Rivas Vasquez / Jaya Bear.
-- 1st ed.
    p. cm.
    LCCN: 99-75819
    ISBN: 0-9674255-0-6

    1. Rivas Vasquez, Agustin. 2. Shamans--Peru--
Biography. 3. Ayahuasca. 4. Indians of South
America--Peru--Medicine. I. Title.

    BF1622.P4B43 2000   299'.8911 [B]
                      QBI99-1420

Printed in the United Stated of America

10   9   8   7   6   5   4   3   2   1

I would like to dedicate this book to the bright spirit of my daughter Brahmani, to my beloved Sun Bear who passed into spirit in 1992, and to my parents Roselyn and Efry Amler.

Acknowledgements

It is with much gratitude that I would like to thank all the people who have helped me in seeing this book come to it's completion; Monica Hernandez and Agnes Chavez who were stalwart with the transcription and translation of tapes from Spanish into English; Carol Parker, Wendy Higgins and Michael Monroney who read parts of the manuscript and offered me positive suggestions and strong support; Shabari Bird and Matthew Ryan who gave technical suggestions which helped me decide on how I would produce this book; Carolyn Boren who has been extremely generous in her willingness to translate legal documents into Spanish; Devin Miller who lightened my load by proof reading; Lynda Ferris who has worked on the cover design and the typography, with a constant positive attitude and willingness to help; Ann Mason and Wabun Wind my two editors, who gave professional and exacting advice, which helped the book come into it's proper form; Ellen Kleiner who has helped with the book's logistics; and Jane Hutchinson who allowed me to use some of her photos. I thank you all.

I also thank Don Agustin Rivas Vasquez for entrusting me to write the story of his life, and for all the support he has given me on this project.

Contents

Preface

A year and a half after my husband Sun Bear died, I settled into a new home in Taos, New Mexico. The events of the past eighteen months had clarified my need to chart a new course in life and to rid myself of emotional and mental patterns keeping me from experiencing a state of inner light and mental clarity. After reading some autobiographical and spiritual accounts of other people's journeys to Peru, I decided to go there myself. I had very pleasant memories from a previous visit when Sun Bear and I had been in the mountain areas of Cuzco and Machu Picchu. I intuitively knew going to Peru would herald a major change in my life.

An acquaintance was taking groups to the Peruvian jungle to work with a shaman and *ayahuasquero*. At the time I knew nothing about *ayahausca* (literally translated as the "rope, or vine, of death"). My intent was to get to Peru, and I knew I needed a powerful experience to shift me out of my present state of "reality."

The group flew to Iquitos where we were met by the shaman Don Agustin Rivas. Our group, consisting of about twenty people, came from all over the United States. I was waiting for our luggage to arrive, and I hadn't met Don Agustin yet, when he approached me and, without knowing anything about me, simply stated, "You are from Taos."

So began a two-week magical encounter. The next morning we journeyed up the Amazon river for three hours in a motor-driven, forty-foot-long canoe-like boat, covered with a thatched roof. Traveling along, we were blissfully unaware of how deceptive the dull gray, apparently peaceful Amazon River is. In fact, it has very fierce currents and powerful forces whirling through it's great depths. All along the banks, as we passed small villages and gatherings of huts, the people were bathing, washing clothes, and generally using this giant serpent of a river in their

daily lives, regardless of how polluted it now is. Children sat a-
long its banks, played in it, or stood outside their houses and
waved greetings to us.

Finally we arrived at a little village called Tamshiyacu. Crowds
of villagers flocked to the shore to greet us, and children surrounded the boat, then clambered aboard. Everyone vied for the
opportunity of carrying our luggage, as this is one of their few
sources of income. Disembarking, we began a one and a half hour
walk into the jungle to Don Agustin's retreat called, "Yushintaita",
which he has built in typical jungle style with open-sided,
thatched-roof houses on stilts.

The time we spent with Don Agustin, over the next two weeks,
included working with the visionary plant medicine *ayahuasca*,
which is a part of the healing and spiritual tradition of the
Peruvian Amazon. We also did an intense intestinal cleanse with
ojé, another jungle plant, explored the jungle environment around
his encampment, listened to his discourses, and took herbal and
clay baths. While we were there, the *ayahuasca* was prepared
ceremonially over a two day period, and the entire group participated in four deeply transformative *ayahuasca* ceremonies.

Ayahuasca is a plant that has been used for healing in the
Amazon for thousands of years. Before there were hospitals,
clinics and doctors in the area, *ayahuasca* was used to cure
people. Even with all the hospitals today, people still come in
search of shamans to cure them with the help of *ayahuasca* and
other plant medicines. Don Agustin continues to use and
promulgate *ayahuasca*, so that the ceremonies stay alive, and the
historical tradition of this divine medicine is not lost.

The nights of ceremony in the temple in the middle of the
jungle, surrounded by the sounds of all the night creatures —
monkeys howling, frogs croaking, birds calling, the jungle
lushness breathing its rhythm into my rhythm — were magical.
In my first *ayahuasca* ceremony the *ayahuasca* felt like rivers of
golden light going through every nerve in my body, cleansing,
purifying. I experienced a clearing on every level physical, emo-

tional, mental, spiritual — a shift in consciousness through every cell of my body. *Ayahuasca* visions of incandescent lights and geometric patterns surrounded me. I watched as Agustin circled the temple, dancing and singing, beating his drum, resonating his string instruments to a healing vibration for each person he passed, tuning into their frequency and balancing and harmonizing their energy fields with the sounds. Seeing his light body as it stretched out in front of him, and seeing the astral body left behind, I wasn't sure where his body ended, as his shimmering multi-colored energy field passed my line of vision. I closed my eyes and entered into a deeper state, ignoring the thousands of images that flashed before my mind's eye, knowing it was clearing and cleaning the past. An insistent sensation in my stomach temporarily brought me back to a semi-state of body consciousness as I vomited up the *ayahuasca*. The pot I was vomiting into seemed like an endlessly deep well as I saw serpents come pouring out of my mouth, and I knew I had cleaned out more than my physical body. Cleansed I went deeper into the *ayahuasca* vision seeing lights, colors, and imperceptible changes in my molecular structure. *Ayahuasca* filled my body like a slow-moving river — filled it and overflowed, joining the currents that moved through the jungle, joining the sounds of the night. The ceremony continued into the early hours of the morning.

The next morning, after only three hours of sleep, I felt vibrant, alive, incredibly clean as I took a bath in the clean jungle river that flows through Don Agustin's land.

A month after I returned to the United States, Don Agustin called me from New York and invited me to join him there. I packed my bags, and four hours later I was off to Albuquerque to fly out and join him for ten days, using the frequent flyer miles I had accumulated. Over that time he held three ceremonies in different places. I wondered how it would be working with *ayahuasca* outside the jungle, but either because of my strong connection to Agustin and the energy of the jungle he carried with him, or because of my prior *ayahuasca* journeys, all the ceremonies were as powerfully healing as my first experiences.

Two months later I returned to Don Agustin's jungle retreat in Peru, where I spent more time working with him. He told me then that *ayahuasca* never leaves the body. This has proved to be true. I feel the spirit of *ayahuasca* with me, and allow the energy of it to envelop me whenever I choose to tune into its presence.

I eventually started taking my own groups of people to Yushintaita so they too could experience their own personal healing with Don Agustin. Through the ceremonies with *ayahuasca*, and the extraordinary work that he does, I have seen many people go through transformations and healing. To me, working with a *maestro ayahuasquero* of the caliber of Don Agustin Rivas is of prime importance. His knowledge and abilities, and his personal connection to the plant spirits and the spirit of *ayahuasca*, are what give integrity to his work.

This story of his life shows clearly his innate connection and sensitivity to the spirit world, as well as his very practical abilities in the physical. His constant striving for independence, and his amazing resourcefulness under all conditions since childhood, are I believe, what made him the shaman he is.

Throughout his life he has always naturally shifted between worlds. For him the reality of the physical plane of existence and the reality of the spirit world are completely interconnected. The cultural acceptance of the interplay of these two realms of existence was a strong factor in shaping his life.

No one is perfect on this physical plane, and Don Agustin is no exception. However, his love and willingness to help others, and his ability to actually do so, have motivated me to continue my work with him. I have constantly been amazed at the magic and power that come through him during ceremonies. His energy in sharing his love for *ayahuasca* has transformed many people's lives, and also allowed numerous individuals access into a world they would otherwise not have perceived. My own work with Don Agustin has opened a realm of connectedness to the plant spirits, as well as a deeper awareness of my inner light.

I eventually asked Don Agustin if he would allow me to write a book about his life. This book is his story as he narrated it to me. I have kept his voice and way of speaking as much as the translation allowed, and only a few names have been omitted or changed to protect privacy.

Chapter 1
Growing Up in a Jungle Village

I was born on August 28, 1933 in Tamshiyacu, Peru, a small town currently with a population of about 5,000. It is the capital city of the district of Fernando Lores, province of Mainas Loreto, in the Amazon. I was given the name Agustin because my birth occurred on the day of St. Agustin.

My father was a Spanish man, a mechanical engineer who was born in Iquitos, after his parents had come from Santiago de Compostela in Spain. Before my birth he often made trips from Iquitos to Tamshiyacu, trying to court my mother, whose name was Desideria Vasquez Pezo. He would arrive with his guitar and another man. Always drunk, they nevertheless would sing and play the guitar very well. Although my father was very much in love with my mother, my maternal grandparents, being very religious Catholics, were very strict and protective of her, and would not receive him in the house because he was a drunk and always sang mundane songs. He'd serenade my mother in front of the house, and my grandparents would respond by throwing urine at him. Then my father would leave disconsolately, returning by rowboat to Iquitos. At that time there were no motorboats.

The Amazon River was always full of mysteries and dangers. Despite barely escaping death numerous times, my father always returned to see my mother. When he traveled to see her the nights were sometimes very dark and the way obscured by thunderstorms. In addition to facing the river's big waves, there was always the fear of encountering the *Yacurunas*, the spirits that according to the Amazon mythology, lived in the water. Many people disappeared, and it was always said they were carried away by the *Yacurunas*. However there were also many voracious alligators and boas in the river at that time. Despite such potential perils, my father kept returning to see my mother, trying to win her affections.

After a while, my father, who was very intelligent, began singing religious songs to her. Hearing this, my grandfather became more agreeable to his presence. One day as my father was singing during a gathering storm, it started to rain on him and his guitar. My grandfather opened the door and let him enter the house. My grandfather asked him to continue singing inside but never gave him an opportunity to be alone with my mother. Even though the family guarded her carefully, during one visit my father somehow managed to impregnate my mother. Subsequently my sister Maria Antonieta was born in 1931. My sister was very small because during her pregnancy my mother was fearful since it was her first child.

Following this event my father continued coming to Tamshi-yacu to see my mother and my sister. Each time my grandfather would have a party, killing chickens for the meal, expecting my father to marry my mother. Eventually my sister was taken to Iquitos to meet her Spanish grandparents.

When my sister was two years old, my mother got pregnant with me during one of my father's trips. After I was born, my father's Spanish family in Iquitos doubted I was really his son, since I was much darker skinned with many of my mother's characteristics. I looked more like an Inca. My maternal grandparents were descendants of the Inca as well as the Spanish, while my paternal grandparents were Spanish people. Eventually my father's parents ordered him to disappear from Iquitos and go to Brazil, because my maternal grandfather was instigating litigation to get him to acknowledge me as his son, and sign a birth certificate so I would legally have his last name. As a result my father didn't acknowledge me and sign my birth certificate until I was fourteen years old.

During this time my mother lived in Iquitos, while I stayed in Tamshiyacu with my maternal grandparents. My father continued lying to my mother, promising her he would marry her. While she worked making woven furniture, and other preparations for their future house he suddenly married another woman who was also already pregnant by him. After being totally deceived, and learning that he had married this other woman, my mother then returned to Tamshiyacu to take care of me and my sister. Sadly, according to my mother, my father had no interest in what eventually became of her or of his children.

My own first memories are of experiences growing up with my maternal grandparents, especially of seeing my grandfather grinding the sugarcane. My grandparents had a big house in the country with lots of land, where there were gardens, cows, pigs, chickens, dogs, and cats, as well as a *trapiche*, a hand-operated machine that ground sugarcane to make juice which was then fermented to produce an alcoholic drink, or made into a sweet cane syrup, or into hard blocks of dark sugar. It was the epoch of *barbasco*, (a plant containing large amounts of a dangerous substance, rotenone, and used as an insecticide by the Europeans), and everyone in the village planted it. My grandfather cultivated and harvested the *barbasco*, and it was as young children that we began working in agriculture. When I was only six years old, I helped plant pineapples and *barbasco*. Growing up in this agricultural environment I learned much about the care of plants, and thus helped carry on the tradition. Whether there was rain or sun, we had to work on the *chacra* (the plot of land that each family farmed), because if we didn't we couldn't eat.

My mother took very good care of us. I remember her chewing ripe bananas after roasting them in the embers, then like a mother bird does for her young, feeding them to us. I'd consume a large banana by myself, that was my ration of food. When I was an infant, I was breast-fed by my mother, but my first memories of food are of bananas. My mother fed us all kinds of foods, but always after first chewing them which was a customary practice at that time.

We drank the sweet fresh milk of cows that my mother milked by hand, as well as sugarcane juice. My grandfather made this especially for *fiestas* or cultural events in our town.

My grandfather owned three houses. One was the tranquil farm, where I was born and lived during my early childhood, and where the cows, pigs and hens were raised, and where the *trapiche* was kept. Another house was located in the town. Here we later lived, slept, socialized and prayed in the church which my grandfather had created in the house. The third house was on the opposite bank of the Amazon river from Tamshiyacu. The land there was very fertile since it was periodically flooded by waters from the Amazon when it was at its highest level and overflowed its banks. There plantains, *yuca* (a root vegetable that is eaten almost daily by the people of the Amazon), tomatoes, sweet peppers, beans, and rice grew along with sweet delicious papayas, which would not grow in Tamshiyacu because the land was not as fertile.

As a child, I had my own small canoe, which I'd row across the Amazon to the farm, while my grandfather went with my grandmother in a big boat. Although we would leave at the same time, sometimes I'd get to the other side of the river before them, which pleased my grandfather since it showed I was strong.

The Amazon there is three or four kilometers wide. Sometimes there were high winds and big waves, which I learned how to navigate to avoid sinking. When the horizon would sometimes turn black my grandfather would say, "Do you see that black coming? That's a very strong wind." At those times we couldn't cross the river, since the waves were two or three meters high, like the ocean, and it was very dangerous. We'd need to wait until after the storm passed.

I loved going to our farm where the *yuca*, the sugarcane, the corn, and huge plantains grew. Watching the birds — the *paucares*, the *suysuyis* — flying back and forth and eating their fill of fat bunches of plantain, I'd abandon myself to the sweetness of life as only a child can do.

We'd weed the crops and harvest them. In the process we'd

sometimes find poisonous snakes, like the *loromachaco* and the *jeregon*, which we had to kill. Nobody was ever killed by a snake because our eyes where sharp, and we always paid attention to where we put our hands.

In the garden and in the chili tree, there were always small green parrots which I would hit with a little stick that I carried around with me, because they ate the chilies. Then my mother would take my stick away. Being a child and not knowing any better, I also ate the chilies, and then I'd start screaming and crying because they were too hot. But the next day, I'd go back and eat the peppers again.

My mother would bathe me and my sister, Maria Antonieta (Antuca), together in a big metal bowl in which sugarcane juice was collected. While naked and covered with soapsuds, I would look at our bodies and my imagination would start to work. My penis would stand up, and I would play with myself, because it was strange to me that something so little could grow so big. It was a curiosity to me. I would also get an erection when my mother would put soap between my legs to wash me. Consequently by the time I was five years old, I didn't want my mother to bathe me anymore, because I would always get an erection, causing my mother to hit me and tell me that I was a bad boy, although I was innocent.

During the nights I'd hear the spirits whistling, and my mother would tell me they were from the deceased. In our village, when people heard this whistling at night, they'd start trembling in their beds. If they heard it while in the street, they would start vomiting foam, which could result in death. I personally never had any fear of the spirits, and was instead curious to see them. In fact I'd go into the street looking for the spirit which then would stop whistling. Everyone said that I was a very strange child not to be afraid of those spirits.

My mother said I was very intelligent, and inclined to working with all kinds of tools, such as machetes, and wood carving tools.

When I was about eight years old, I took my grandfather's saw to cut some wood. I had difficulty cutting the wood, so I decided to sharpen it on a rock, as if I were filing a knife or machete. But all the saw's teeth wore almost away due to filing and then it wouldn't cut the wood at all. Later when my grandfather wanted to use the saw, he discovered that there were hardly any teeth left on it and calling to my grandmother, "Simona!" and my mother, "Desideria," he asked, "what happened to this saw?"

"I don't know," they replied, and then they asked me if I had done that.

"Yes," I had to admit. My grandfather was very angry, since afterwards it was very difficult to re-sharpen the saw and virtually create new teeth. We had to buy a triangular file that could sharpen the teeth one by one which took a long time.

At age ten, I started school, two years earlier than the customary age at the time. At school most of the children had head lice, and they were transmitted to me. When my mother looked through my hair and found lice, she got very angry and said, "Why did you let the lice get into your hair?" I didn't know how to answer her, because although I wasn't guilty since other children had given me the lice, I could never say anything to her that contradicted what she was saying. Then my mother took the scissors and cut my hair, but not having a razor she did a terrible job, and later I had to go to the barber Vicente Pinche, who shaved my head completely.

When I went back to school, the children made fun of my head. They painted skulls on their hands, and said to me, "Hello, my mirror friend," and then with the skulls painted on their hands, stamped my bald head. After I returned home, my mother became angry when she saw the skulls painted on it, along with the words *on credit*. But I couldn't tell her I wasn't guilty.

"You have two, three skulls on your head! Why did you let them paint on your head?"

"I didn't see them do it mother."

"And why does it say on credit? You always pay for things, you never take things on credit!"

As a result my mother made me a hat with a cord to cover my head, but the kids still pulled it off and teased me. However in spite of this, I did very well in school. I was intelligent and listened to my teacher. When the end of the year came I was always the best student and passed on to the next level, while many of the children who had hassled me had to repeat grades.

My grandfather was the most religious man in the town. I grew up in a Catholic environment, with many religious figurines. Since there was no longer a formal church in Tamshiyacu, my grandfather's house became the church. He would preside over church services, and perform marriage ceremonies and baptisms. The original town church had been damaged by cows that had gotten into it and destroyed most of the saints and the door of the church — it was a very poor church. Afterward my grandfather put the remaining statues on a large table in his house, including statues of the Virgin Mary, Jesus Christ, Saint Santiago, the Virgin Purisima, and the Nativity. Priests would also occasionally come from Iquitos to preside over mass, baptisms, marriages, and confirmations. On such occasions they would pray with their rosaries and do liturgies all night, making my grandfather very happy.

The Nativity Virgin is the patron saint of my town, and the annual festival in her honor on September 8 is the main local celebration. The festivities are not as elaborate now as they used to be. Formerly devotees who celebrated them would prepare for an entire month before the occasion. Even though Tamshiyacu has grown, today the festivity for the patron saint has diminished in quality, because the people now celebrate with electronic music, and pay tribute to the virgin only until eleven at night then they start partying. In the past the ceremony was more spiritually elevated with the priests impressively dressed in white cassocks with black waistbands. I remember loving the ceremony and wanting to join the priests. When I was a little older, my grandfather sent me away to a seminary in Iquitos, so I could study to be a priest.

For as long as I can remember, I have always had a love of music. I remember that I used to put little metal plates in the drawers of a table, then pound on them to make sounds like a piano or a marimba while the other children gathered in front of my house to listen.

When I was ten I helped my grandfather farm *barbasco* (also called *rotanona* or *cube*), a poisonous plant. The English and Americans bought the plant in huge quantities, and used the root to produce insecticides. The price of the plant was very high at that time, and everyone in the town, aware of its value, cleared huge sections of the jungle to plant it. But after three or four years the price came down, and people were disappointed because they had to sell it at 70 or 80 *centavos* per kilo, instead of the 2.50 *soles* received previously. They also lost out because many of them had gotten rid of all their *humarales*, a fruit that grows here in the jungle, to plant *barbasco*.

For a while I gathered *barbasco* roots to sell and received 70 *centavos* per kilo, which was a lot of money. In a day I'd make about 40 *soles*, since I could harvest 60 to 70 kilos a day. Since in those days there were no horses or cars, we'd carry the plants on our heads for two or three hours to sell them at market. Fortunately even at that young age I was a strong young boy and I could carry a heavy weight.

My grandfather would stash all the money made from *barbasco* inside two big trunks, which had locks that would ring seven times if someone tried to open them. My uncle, Julio Vasquez, my mother's brother, was the only person entrusted to count the money with my grandfather, which they did from three to five in the morning. I would hear them because at three I'd sometimes get up to pee, and at five we got up to pray. Then we'd go to the land with my grandfather, where the cows, pigs, and hens were.

One day there was a big fire in town, and houses made of leaves were burning quickly. The fire was spreading toward my grandfather's house. Meanwhile, my grandfather, strengthened by his resolve to save the trunks filled with silver coins, carried them out of the house by himself, along with all the saints and religious statues, since everyone else, even the army, was involved in helping to stop the fire.

Eventually the fire was contained before our house was burned. Then my grandfather couldn't bring the trunks back because they were too heavy. It took five people to bring everything back, using a stick as leverage. The next day people found burnt pigs and hens in the fire's ashes. Nearly all the people in the town had lost all their belongings.

Very early the day after the fire, my grandfather called me to pray, telling me that it had been the will of God and the saints that our house was the only one in town that had not been destroyed. We knelt and prayed all morning, until my knees hurt.

In 1947 or 1948 when I was fifteen, the famous Zatipo mud slide occurred in the Amazon River. A huge avalanche of mud flowed to the Amazon, carrying with it broken trees, dead cows, dead people, and houses floating with their roofs of leaves. During that time it was impossible to sail on the river as the danger was far greater than usual. Even under ordinary conditions the Amazon can be very dangerous, especially when it is windy. You can see the kind of wind that's coming by the color of the sky. If it's a blue color, then it's a smooth wind, and the waves are small. But if there's a black cloud approaching, then the situation is very dangerous and it is necessary to get off the river. Sometimes there are winds that come from both sides, creating tall waves that rise crazily all over the place, but it's more dangerous when a wind comes from only one direction. Then boats have to sail quickly to shore because the resulting huge waves can sink them easily. Even though the Amazon may appear tranquil at times, there are whirlpools and terrible currents that have the power to pull huge rocks down into its depths. Also, living deep inside the

Amazon are incredible boas, one or two meters in diameter (three to six feet) and twelve to thirty meters (forty to one hundred feet) long that normally never come out. If a person drowns, the boas swallow them, so the corpse doesn't come up to the surface at all. However during the Zatipo mud slide, in order to survive, the boas came out of the river, while the dolphins got into the lakes. Some smaller fishes also survived by getting into drain pipes where the lakes drain into the river, but most of them died by suffocating from lack of oxygen in the mud. It was a terrible time but, again, our family was spared.

My grandfather was also a *shiringuero* (rubber tapper), who extracted rubber used for car tires. At that time a big business in Iquitos was the extraction of rubber milk from trees, and the formation of it into balls for export to England, Europe, and the United States. Foreigners also came in search of mahogany and animal skins, killing millions and millions of *huanganas* (wild boars), *sajinos* (jungle pigs), deer, and alligators, removing their skins, and taking the hides to the United States and Europe. As a result of overhunting and deforestation, today almost all the animals have disappeared from the region, and the mahogany has been destroyed as well. The people responsible for this destruction are not people from the Amazon, but foreign buyers from England, China, Italy and the United States. So a major problem now is how to preserve the potentially eternal beauty of the Amazon amidst the ever-increasing pressures on the area from farmers, peasants, and hunters. Some animals no longer exist at all, while *otorongos* (jaguars), *majases* (nocturnal animals similar to a huge rodent and good to eat), armadillos, *pucacungas* (birds similar to hens), the *paujil* (a black wild turkey with a red beak), and the *piurí* (a similar kind of bird), have all virtually disappeared. Animals have not been respected, and many times they have been killed while carrying offspring. Also in the rivers and lakes many fish have disappeared.

Instead of having disregard for the environment, we Amazonians need to learn how to breed various species and provide animal and bird sanctuaries to protect the wild jungle animals, like they do in Europe and the United States. To learn such conservation techniques we need the assistance of Europe and the United States.

Also as a result of altered customs and new technology, life in the Amazon has changed in other ways as well. Since with new technology people now have water in town they don't need to go to the river. In the past it was always a beautiful sight to see young girls, with their straight backs, carrying the ceramic water jars on their heads over coiled pieces of cloth. However, men do still carry the produce from their land in wooden boxes on their backs, with the weight on their foreheads distributed by a band attached to the box on their backs. It's astonishing to see how much weight they are able to carry, but over time it takes a toll creating a hole in their skull which can be felt. By contrast, the women who carried vessels or baskets on their heads filled with pineapples, *humarís* (a jungle fruit), or water, didn't damage their skulls because they held their heads up and walked straight.

I know how to carry a vessel on my head, as all children were taught when I was a child. One day I was carrying a pot on my head, without holding onto it, and it fell onto the ground. I had to take the pieces back home so that my mother could make a new vessel by grinding them up again and mixing them with more fresh clay and *apacharama* — a tree bark burned to charcoal — to produce a better consistency.

After I broke the jar my mother was angry and hit me with a belt and scraped the skin on my arm with a piece of the broken clay pot until my arm bled — to teach and impress on me to never again break a pot.

When I was about eleven I became fascinated with guns. At the house my grandfather had a carbine rifle that had to be loaded with gunpowder and shells. Returning home after school, while my grandfather was still at his farm, I'd fill his gun with gunpowder and a substance from a tree to hold the gunpowder in, then with BB pellets and more of the glue-like substance. Finally

I'd shoot at the fruits on the trees, managing to hit quite a few, and with the resin dripping from the green fruit I'd be thrilled because I was a good shot. I did this frequently until one day my grandfather was preparing to go hunting and discovered some of his gunpowder had been used and the gun wasn't clean, something he always did after using it.

He was very angry, and shouted, "Who's been using my rifle?"

"I have, grandfather," I confessed sheepishly.

"Why have you used the gun? You're too young to be using it. You're going to kill somebody using this gun!"

"No, grandfather. I'm going to be a great hunter!"

As a result of using my grandfather's rifle I was severly punished. Not by my grandfather, but at dawn by my grandmother who came to my bed with my grandfather's big belt. I was very strong and tried to get away from her but to no avail. She beat me with the belt. Then when I jumped under the bed, she poked at me with a broom. I grabbed the end of the broom, and pulled it, forcing my grandmother under the bed with me. After that she didn't beat me again and told my grandfather that he had to be the one to punish me. I was very mischievous at the time.

In those times, there were lots of animals in the jungle, large fowl, *majases*, and *añujes* (small animals similar to *majases* but day animals). By age eleven I was already hunting animals for food.

In the evenings I'd play with my friends in the street or, when I was older, visit my girlfriend. I'd also read, or play music with my drum, while my grandfather played the flute. In addition I participated in various festivals each year, like the big festivity on September 7 and 8, where we would dance all night to drum and flute music. Because I always played the drum at these festivities, we practiced music almost every night.

Whenever my grandfather had the responsibility of one celebration, a month before it we'd go into the jungle near Tamshiyacu to a place where many animals came for water and fruit. There we'd hunt, to feed the patrons of the festival. The Spanish Agustin priests from Iquitos attended these festivities, and when they arrived my grandfather gave them his full attention. We prepared comfortable beds and good food, while the town's people cooked sweets, bread, corn, and *yuca*. When the festivities started on the night of September 7, there was a procession of the Nativity Virgin during which I would play the drum and my grandfather would play the flute.

During our childhood, my sister and I were generally healthy. Whenever it rained all the children in the town would bathe in the streets. Sometimes we'd eat only once a day — eating whatever was available, plantains, *yuca* or bread. People in the poor villages usually ate what they grew themselves or whatever wild plants were available. We were happy living without pollution, factories, cars, television, and the other distractions of city life. In the evenings we'd play games or sing and fall asleep tired and dirty with our clothes on. We didn't have sheets to cover ourselves so when it was cold we'd huddle together with our mothers for warmth. Despite our poverty and sometimes lack of food, it seemed like we were nourished by the clean air and natural environment.

Sometimes I'd skip school and go with a group of boys to the Amazon or the gorge of flowers to swim. At that time, Tamshiyacu had a beautiful gorge with crystalline cold water, and we'd swim there for hours in the afternoon until our eyes were red. When I'd return home, my mother and grandfather would look at me and know immediately I hadn't gone to school, and I'd be spanked with a folded leather belt.

In those days all the kids swam nude together without feeling self-conscious, whereas now kids wear clothes and are ashamed. Being playful, we'd touch the girls under water, making them run away. There wasn't any sexual intent behind these actions at our age of nine or ten; we were just being naughty and teasing the girls. We'd still swim like this even when we were fifteen to sixteen-years old.

Often at night after supper, a group of girls and boys would play *pam-pam visto*, a game of hide-and-seek in the jungle. Since we had grown up in the jungle environment, we never worried about the snakes nor the *chambira* tree's spines, even though the spines would penetrate the thick skin on the soles of our bare feet. The next day we'd help each other remove them with knives. Some of the spines were a half inch long and would sometimes break off inside. My grandfather, who never wore shoes, didn't even feel the spines; his feet were as tough as shoe soles and looked like horse feet.

Chapter 2
Sorcery

One time my mother had a spell put on her by a *brujo*, a sorcerer who used black magic against her because she didn't want to go to bed with him. She felt as though a spine or dart had stuck in her liver. She was in great pain.

To remedy the situation my grandfather, taking six men with him, went to get a very good friend named Pancho Oroma, who was the most famous Amazonian *banco*, a shaman of the highest level. He lived far away, above Tapira, where he had a clinic to cure numerous sick people. After six hours on the river my grandfather arrived at Pancho Oroma's house, and told him, "Friend, your god child, Desideria, is feeling very bad. She has terrible pain. She says that she's been bewitched."

"There are many *brujos* now, and they're putting bad spells on a lot of people. But those cheap *brujos* can't do anything against me. I can kill them if I want," Pancho Oroma said.

"Then come with me to see Desideria," said my grandfather.

Pancho Oroma told my grandfather, "I'll be leaving soon. You go first and maybe I'll arrive before you."

My grandfather said, "Come with me and we can go quickly."

"No, don't worry, my friend. I will go the way I know," the shaman responded.

I had stayed at home with my mother, who kept me and my sister awake all night with her constant suffering. Suddenly we heard a sound above the house, on the roof. There was a huge owl with an enormous head looking at us, almost as if it were a person. Scared, I closed my mosquito net to hide from it. Eventually, we saw it fly down and transform into Pancho Oroma as it touched the floor. It made me laugh, because I had never seen a big bird fly down and transform itself into a man.

"Desideria, I came to heal you child. Where does it hurt you?" asked the shaman.

"Oh father, here, by the ribs, and I can't stand the pain," moaned my mother.

"You need to be brave, and I'll heal you," Pancho Oroma said, then gargled and made some phlegm come out of his throat. After sucking her with it, he swallowed whatever came out of her, then reassured her saying, "Okay daughter, you're all right now."

"Yes, it doesn't hurt anymore," my mother answered. We were astonished that the pain had disappeared so quickly.

"You won't have any more pain, child. Now I am going," the shaman said, and after transforming back into an owl, he flew up and left.

My mother was very happy because of the shaman's healing, and we all went to sleep peacefully. About two hours later, my grandfather showed up and said, "Blast! my friend hasn't come."

"Yes he did come," said my mother.

"Did he heal you?"

"Yes, it doesn't hurt me anymore."

Don Pancho Oroma was a powerful shaman. He could kill just by looking at a person. After sucking the ailment out of my mother, he sent the illness back to the sorcerer who had bewitched my mother, killing him.

Afterwards, sitting on our beds, my sister and I started laughing about the sounds Pancho Oroma had made while he was healing our mother, getting the *yachai*, the phlegm, out of his throat. As children we thought it was funny to see him spitting the phlegm on our mother's body. My mother, however, found our laughter annoying since she had just experienced a miraculous healing.

This firsthand experience with a *banco* left a deep impression on me. I have the desire to be a *banco* at this time in my life, but I lack the necessary resolution because of all of the work I am involved in, and all the people who come to me for help. I would have to be away from my woman for a year, living alone in the jungle and following a very rigorous diet, eating nothing but rice and plantains, and occasionally monkeys from the jungle. It is through such a discipline that one can reach the level of *banco*, gaining the power to fly with speed and skill, transforming into and using the vehicles of water — alligators, boas, and dolphins — or the vehicles of the air — owls, *manshacos* (type of heron or stork with smooth, silvery gray feathers), hummingbirds, *catalans* (little birds that dive into the water and catch fish), *shararas* (birds similar to a duck which catch fish), and *wapapas* (nocturnal birds that eat fish). All these animals, all these birds, can be vehicles for the *brujo*, the sorcerer, or the healer. For me *brujo* is the right word. Back then the word shaman wasn't known, only now we know the word. Earlier we were all *brujos*, some doing good and some doing evil. Originally *brujos* performed both good and evil deeds, since almost nobody would do only good. At that time if people paid a *brujo* well to do evil, he would agree.

In past times, elders would drink *ayahuasca* to have visions and to gain knowledge about the different plant medicines. When my grandfather drank *ayahuasca*, he could see visions of what he needed to do, whether it was cultivate the farm or fix the roads. Once it was seen through the *ayahuasca* visions what public work was needed, the governors of each town and district would gather their people together to do it. All the people were very strong and could carry enormous trees. Thirty to forty people would carry one huge tree, using poles to bolster the tree from underneath, with people on each side to balance the weight. To encourage work the supervisors would prepare *masato* for the workers, a beer made from the juice of *yuca* or sugarcane, ground in my grand- father's *trapiche*, and then fermented over four days. While the work was going on musical bands would play typical marches or individual musicians would play the flute and drums, and everyone would sing and shout while they worked. In rain or shine they continued working. Since my grandfather played the flute very well, when public construction was underway, such as the building of bridges, he would play the flute. I would sometimes accompany him with the drum, which I played well.

Although the work was arduous, it was done in a beautiful, tropical landscape. The *papagayos* or *guacamayos* (birds with a crown of yellow, blue and red feathers), the toucans and the parrots flying around would adorn the blue Amazon sky with their brilliant colors, and the winds would provide fresh breezes. Even though people would get wet with rain, they wouldn't feel cold. The people were *chuchuhuasheros*, individuals made strong through drinking the medicine made from the bark of the *chuchuhuasha* tree, which they would mix with rum made from sugarcane. In those days they would make good rum not like that made today. Now rum is mixed with lots of chemicals and acids that cause people to die of ulcers or possibly cancer.

During the entire time I was growing up, my whole family — my mother, uncles, and grandparents — all drank *ayahuasca* and participated in the ceremonies. In this manner they were able to gain direct knowledge about their culture. *Ayahuasca*, which was a central part of everyone's lives, was like a television set where we could see clearly what was necessary to do in the future. Any person who drinks this powerful plant, which has existed over many generations, and was possibly brought from other planets, also has the ability to travel through space, not only using the human form but also the forms of birds or animals.

In our visions, we can see snakes like boas, colors, lights, and spirits who come to heal. In *ayahuasca* ceremonies, very sick individuals are placed lying down within a mosquito net to be healed. You can see the spirits when they come to the mosquito net to heal the people. There are many stories about the cures that have taken place during such ceremonies.

Ayahuasca ceremonies were done in different places and everyone was friends with the *ayahuasqueros*, the individuals who conducted *ayahuasca* ceremonies. Some families based their lives on their visions, from which they learned how to heal, and how to use various plants to promote health. Some people decorated ceramics with designs from their visions. In those days all the kitchen utensils were made by the people who used them.

Today I continue to promulgate and use *ayahuasca* to keep the ceremonies alive. I don't want the historical tradition of this divine medicine to be lost.

The use of native plants to promote health and healing was widely practiced. All of us were healthy because we lived in a wonderful natural environment with no radios, televisions, or electricity, and we maintained good health by going to bed early and getting up at four or five in the morning.

Every morning my grandparents drank a small cup of *chuchuhuasha* or *chiriqsanango*, powerful plant tonics that gave strength and health. After dawn, with the sun shining brilliantly like gold in the east, and with the birds, the *suysuyis*, the *paucares*, the herons and the toucans saluting the new day with their songs, we would eat and then start off to work at the farm where pineapples, *yuca*, plantains, and other fruits were cultivated.

On the weekends and after school, I would help my grandfather plant his land. At that time, *barbasco*, a poison, had a good selling price, and everyone planted it for export since boats arrived from England and Panama to get it. My grandfather also had large pineapple plants and large *humarí* trees — bearing a black fruit that is harvested in February. When it's the season for *humarí*, everyone in the village gathers it. You eat the thin, greasy outer part, which tastes like butter. It can be eaten with bread or made into a good oil. My grandfather was very thrifty and instead of buying grease from the hardware store he would make his own from *humarí* to use on the *trapiche*. Throughout my childhood I continued to learn and gain knowledge about various aspects of agriculture.

Although it was possible to get wet and cold walking through the dewy dawn, we were able to ward off sickness by drinking *ayahuasca*, *sanango*, or *chuchuhuasha*, and thus retained good health. We learned how to use these medicines as children, as well as how to heal with plants. There were no hospitals and doctors then, so we all used what nature provided.

When we had colic or stomach aches, my mother or grandparents would give us the juice from the leaves of the red *achiote* fruit, as well as placing a cloth soaked in urine on our bellies, and the pain would immediately subside. When we had parasites we were given *ojé*, the latex from a tree, to drink. When children got indigestion, mothers would give them *piñisma* or hen excrement. Vomiting was induced by using *verbena* or *ñuqñupichana* with *piñisma* and pounded cockroaches, or urine (usually the grandmother's urine, which stinks). This concoction was horrible for children and caused them to vomit.

From time to time an epidemic of whooping cough would come to our villages, causing kids to cough so hard all night long, that it sounded like their lungs were breaking into pieces. When we had a cough, or whooping cough, my mother would prepare the very bitter plants *ñuqñupichana* or *verbena*, by grinding a small amount of their leaves to extract one or two spoonfuls of the juice. With a corn husk between our teeth, it would take four or five people to squeeze our noses and make us drink this potion. Then we'd immediately start vomiting, and the cough would completely stop. Another cure for whooping cough was *verbena* mixed with urine and a black soap that came from Brazil called *yacaré*. They would melt the soap to provoke vomiting and stop the cough.

Since there were no hospitals or medical posts, apart from the generally known plant cures, the *brujos* or sorcerers were the physicians who cured the people. They saved many lives.

Many illnesses are caused by the tropical environment of the Amazon, and some of them are known through our grandparent's traditions. One of these is called *chirapa*, or *shikshi* which occurs when a rainbow has formed in the sky, and at the same time there is still a fine rain falling. It is told that if this rain happens to touch a wound, cut, or scar on a person's body, it can cause inflammation or infection in that area. Likewise, if there is a puddle on the ground containing this powerful substance from the rainbow, and one steps into it with any small wounds or cuts on the feet, it will cause the feet to become swollen and inflamed.

I remember the time of my uncle's wake. My uncle, Alejandro Vasquez had been bitten by a snake on his little toe. At the time it didn't affect him negatively, because he drank *cocona*, an acid fruit, with lots of water, and so didn't need other medicine. He also went to a *brujo* for a cure. My uncle was a young man, and he continued having sex with his wife after the snakebite — something that supposedly could cause death before one has completely healed. One day my uncle went to work without shoes on, tripped over a root, hit the bitten toe, and it got infected. Apparently, as a result, the poison was reactivated, and his leg started swelling. People said it had happened because he was having sex with his wife after the snakebite. In any case, nobody could cure him and he died. Before dying, he asked for some fermented sugarcane juice, which my grandfather always made. We ran to get some, but by the time we came back to town my uncle had already died. At his wake people danced to music in front of the dead body, while my friends and I were in the kitchen trying to drink some of the sugarcane liquor.

The elders of the village knew how to cure snakebites. If you can catch a snake right away after the attack and kill it, you are more likely to be cured. While if you let the snake go, you could die. This is because you can use the snakeskin to help cure yourself by covering over with it, the part that the snake has bitten. If bitten, first you tie something around the arm or leg to prevent the blood from moving towards the heart. Then using a knife to cut the area, you suck out the poisoned blood, chewing jungle tobacco first to prevent the poison from penetrating into your teeth or into any lesion in your mouth. If your mouth isn't healthy you had better not do it. You have to suck the bite right away, since if you wait too long the victim will die. Finally you cover the cut with the snakeskin. Afterwards you drink sweet *cocona* juice or sugarcane juice to counteract the effects of the poison. In the case of my uncle's snakebite, he died because the bite was so small it was practically invisible, and so no one sucked out the poison. The snake that bit him, called *cascabel*, was very small, about thirty centimeters long, but was extremely poisonous. Many times *ayahuasqueros* would sing their magical songs for people with snakebites, but most times this wouldn't cure them.

Chapter 3
Yacurunas: Spirits of the Amazon

One night when I was about eleven, I woke during the night because I had to urinate. There was a full moon, and the night was so clear you could read a book by its light. There was no wind, and it was so silent one couldn't even hear the whistling of the *difuntos*, the spirits of the deceased, nor the dogs barking. Silence and light permeated the village.

I didn't want to go into the forest to pee, so instead looked for a place closer. Around the house my grandfather had built a fence, with narrow wooden planks. There were some spaces in between the narrow planks through which I could pee into the street.

While standing there, I could hear voices, but I couldn't understand what they were saying. I stopped peeing, looked through the space in the fence, and saw two white forms with long robes approach and pass by.

Because the night was so clear and the moon so bright, I could see that they weren't standing on the ground but were about one foot above the ground. The two tall figures were holding hands, and moved in the air. Not observing my presence behind the fence, they conversed in a strange language that seemed to consist of guttural sounds rather than words.

I wasn't afraid, so I opened the gate to observe the figures better. They were already about forty meters away, but I decided to follow them. I went out the gate, closing it very lightly so I could get in again. There was a shadow running along the fence, and silently in that shadow I followed them. Strangely, no dogs barked at me, which I took as a sign that Nature wanted me to have this experience.

After two blocks, I could hear someone performing an *ayahuasca* ceremony, and I could hear them singing the *mariris*, the magical songs. I remembered that a family by the name of Gomez lived nearby, and that this family customarily performed *ayahuasca* ceremonies. They were the most famous *brujos* in Tamshiyacu, and they were great healers. Since there were no hospitals in Tamshiyacu at that time, they took the responsibility for whatever healing emergency was needed.

The two spirits entered into this house. I am sure there was someone with a grave illness there that night. I remained about twenty meters in front of the house behind a small *guayaba* tree, where I waited for about ten minutes, with numerous mosquitoes attacking every bare area on my body. Preferring to resist their bites rather than move, I remained quietly hidden behind the tree and with my eyes glued to the front of the house. The buzzing of the mosquitoes along with the sound of the *mariris* coming from the ceremony intensified the contrasting silence of the night. The moon's clear silver-white light made everything stand out in silhouette.

Suddenly the two figures came out, passing right through the door without opening it. They started to return by the same path they had come, and I followed them at a distance. In awe I watched them float in the air some twelve inches above the ground as they walked holding hands. I continued to follow the spirits past my house in the direction of the Amazon River, where I watched as they went down the sandbank to the shore. There were still no dogs, and nothing was interfering with my investigation. Above on the hill, I watched them throw themselves into the river. At that moment the water made a sound like a whirlpool, and then the two spirits disappeared.

I was familiar with the mythology of the *Yacurunas*, since my grandfather talked about it when I was boy. He told me there were the *Yacurunas*, the spirits that live beneath the waters of all the rivers, wherever there is a place of silence, where they cannot be disturbed with the energy of electrical technology. They are great doctors who can cure illnesses not treatable through medical science, and they can be summoned through ceremonies to heal the sick. When we are doing a ceremony with *ayahuasca* and there are ill people, the *Yacurunas* come to cure these people when we sing the *mariris*. Then it is certain the ill person will be cured.

People say the *Yacurunas* have their heads turned around backwards and that they can never look forwards. When they abduct a person, they immediately turn that individual's head around to face the back so that the person cannot return home and will instead continue to go further and further away into their city deep in the Amazon River. After they can trust the abducted person, they then change the individual's head to face the front again. By that time the person has already learned how to heal, then they can leave.

According to the mythological tradition, there are also healers called *Sirenas*, creatures who have the body of a beautiful woman with long, golden hair and the tail of a fish. The vehicles they use for travel are dolphins, alligators, large turtles, and boas. This mythology is depicted in the paintings of Pablo Amaringo, a contemporary Peruvian artist who paints visionary paintings through his *ayahuasca* experiences, and also in Greek mythology. Around the world different mythological traditions acknowledge the power of eagles, condors, snakes and other animals. Shamans can also transform themselves into animals or birds such as owls, condors, or eagles, so they can travel anyplace to heal.

After the two *Yacurunas* disappeared into the Amazon, I sat on the sidewalk in front of a house thinking about what had happened. At some point I fell asleep. When I awoke the next morning I was in my bed, and couldn't remember when or how I'd gotten to my house, which was three blocks away. I don't remember walking or entering the house, but only awakening when my grandfather called me for morning prayers. At that point I was very sleepy, and he reprimanded me because I wasn't paying attention. It had never happened to me before, since I always got up very early when my grandfather called me to recite prayers. I was always alert. He would wake us every morning at 5:00, and we would kneel in front of the house altar containing the saints and virgins, praying "The Lord's Prayer" as well as other prayers for about half an hour.

Then at sunrise, around 5:30 we'd go to my grandfather's land, called Nuevo Tarapoto, where I was born and where we kept the cows, pigs, and chickens. There we'd make breakfast over a fire built by my grandmother with thick wood. This wood would keep the fire going for days at a time, so that they wouldn't have to waste kerosene and matches to keep lighting it. They'd make the coffee, which we'd sweeten with cane sugar that my grandfather had ground in his *trapiche*.

The morning after I'd seen the *Yacurunas* my grandfather asked me why I was so sleepy so I told him the story. He became afraid and said, "How did you dare follow them? They certainly were *Yacurunas*. That's why they were walking like that, and that's why they went to the place where they were having the *ayahuasca* ceremony. Maybe you interrupted their healing work."

"No, grandfather! They didn't see me, even when I saw them disappear into the water," I answered.

My grandfather responded, "Of course! They disappeared in the Amazon River, as that's where they live. But it's a miracle you didn't disappear in the water also, since you fell asleep right there! Then you would never have come back, and we would never have known where you were!" As punishment for my adventures, he told my grandmother to beat me that night.

That night I slept with a lot of clothes on, so that it wouldn't hurt when my grandmother came to beat me. I awoke when she was near my bed with a big belt. First she admonished me, saying, "Why were you following those *Yacurunas*? They could have stolen you!" Then she started to beat me, but I pulled the belt away from her, screamed and jumped under the bed. Finally she went to bed.

Because news got around quickly in our small village, the next day all the neighbors knew that my grandmother had beaten me.

Like all the small villages along the Amazon River, our town was very poor. The houses were built very close together, constructed of wood with dirt floors, and usually with only two or three rooms. You could always hear what was going on around you in other houses or on the street. Despite slow development, it's essentially the same way today, although now some of the houses have concrete floors and there is electricity from 6:30 until 10:30 at night.

As in any small town, in Tamshiyacu everyone had to express their opinion about the incidents of other people's lives.

Chapter 4
Spirits and Omens

I saw a spirit one day on my grandfather's land. My sister and I had left school to have lunch at Nuevo Tarapoto, which was about half a kilometer from town. The house was situated on an incline, where the *aguajes* grew, the palms that give fruit. We'd go there very early each morning, and sometimes we'd sleep there. This is where my grandfather had the *trapiche*, with which he ground the sugarcane. It was pulled by a *sachavaca*, a tapir which is strong like a horse.

On this day we returned to have lunch while my grandparents were still in the field. When they weren't there, they would leave food prepared for me and my sister, Maria Antonieta. We saw that my uncle, Carlos Mori, who was a police sergeant, was standing by the *trapiche* in his uniform, lifting the cover, as if he were inspecting it. My grandfather used to cover it, to prevent small animals and cockroaches from getting into it.

From about twenty meters away we called to him, and he smiled at us. We wondered what our uncle was doing at the farm, but my sister surmised that he must be resting.

Close by, on the edge of the road there was a cashew tree, with the sweet, pleasing red fruits. Although the birds, the *suysuyís*, usually eat them, strangely that day they weren't eating. Since it was the first time we'd seen this tree with fruit, we ran to pick them. We took two cashews each, and began to suck them — they were juicy and sweet. Then we looked again at the *trapiche* but my uncle wasn't there so I said to my sister, "Uncle is playing with us. He's certainly hiding. Let's go into the house."

The house was an open structure, with a thatched roof and a wire fence to keep the cows from entering it — the way houses in the jungle are generally built. Not seeing my uncle, we called to him, but he didn't answer. I told my sister to look for him in the kitchen, which was about thirty meters away — built as a separate structure so that in the case of a fire the main house and the *trapiche* wouldn't burn. The bedrooms had a fence and a door, but the *trapiche* was a large open room where one could walk in a circle pushing the wheel to grind the sugarcane. My sister went to the kitchen to look while I went to the bedrooms and looked under the woven palm beds made of matting or *bagasse*, which is the residue that is left after the juice has been extracted from the sugarcane. My grandfather would weave that *bagasse*, and that's what we would sleep on, laying down a sheet. We didn't have mattresses, no one used mattresses. We would all sleep on these beds, which were three to four meters wide, and the big ones had mosquito nets.

Perhaps my uncle had hidden there to play with us! But we could not find him anywhere. Suddenly, as I was looking for my uncle, I felt a shudder run through my body, and I left running. My sister also came running out of the kitchen saying, "He's not here, and my body is shivering."

At that point we knew we had seen a spirit and we started running back to the town, to where my uncle lived with his wife. When we arrived my uncle had recently returned from the police station and had been lying down to rest until the lunch was ready. We said, "Uncle, we saw you at Nuevo Tarapoto, inspecting the *trapiche*."

"Get out of here, you're crazy to tell such a story," he responded.

"But we did see you uncle," we insisted.

Then my Aunt Isabelle Vasquez asked, "You saw Carlos?"

"Yes," we said again. She then became very sad, because if someone sees the spirit of an individual, it means that person whose spirit is seen is going to die.

"They must have seen your spirit," our aunt said to our uncle.

"Well, I guess that means I'm going to die," he replied. After that we remained silent, and listened to the family's apprehensive comments about the incident.

Our Uncle Carlos died six years later.

I believe that a person's spirit walks from the moment we're born, because from the moment that we're born we begin to die. Man is condemned to die. So one's spirit is already walking. Nightly sleep is symbolic of death. In the state of rest or sleep, the spirit breaks free, and can leave the body and appear in a physical form in another place. This accounts for why I saw the spirit of my uncle who was resting in the town.

People in Europe and in the United States have seen me appear many times. While they're doing an *ayahuasca* ceremony or during other rituals, they've seen me appear at their ceremonial table.

I liked to go fishing with my uncle Julio Vasquez, my mother's brother. We'd go at night, when there were many fish and huge eight to ten meter-long black alligators in the lakes. Many people wouldn't go fishing out of fear of being eaten by these beasts.

One night I went fishing with uncle Julio, my cousin Ramon, and Julio Vazquez, my uncle Julio's son. I was the youngest of our group, and they placed me on the stern to guide the boat. When we focused our flashlights on the lake water, we could see hundreds of shining alligator eyes. By measuring the distance between the eyes, we could figure out the size of the alligators, some of which were were humongous.

We fished and fished with our net. My uncle was in the prow throwing the net overboard, and I fell asleep, forgetting to guide the boat. My cousin Ramon came to the stern and pushed me overboard to wake me up. When an alligator hears anything fall into the water, it immediately comes to eat it. As soon as I fell in the water, I jumped back up on the boat as quickly as I could. This cured my sleepiness, and I stayed in the stern acting as guide until we had filled the boat up with fishes and left for our campsite to wait until dawn.

Early in the morning we cut and salted the fish, while the huge alligators, smelling the fish blood, lingered like hungry dogs on the shore, waiting for the fish viscera or small discarded fishes.

My Uncle Carlos, in his job as a policeman, took care of the lake. One day he found an Indian fishing without a permit, so he took his lance and harpoon away from him. The Indian was unhappy about this, and cast a spell on my uncle. As a result, little holes appeared on Uncle Carlos's buttocks which itched unbearably. They looked as if they had been caused by worms, but they probably had been caused by nerves.

Another uncle, Ramon Vasquez, my mother's brother, was an *ayahuasquero* and a famous *brujo*. On a stormy day with thunder and lightening, he made a mistake by challenging the *Chullachaqui*, the powerful guardian spirit and master of the jungle. He met up with the *Chullachaqui* in the jungle near Tamshiyacu, and after a fight, the spirit killed my uncle.

When my uncle didn't come home, everyone was worried. Many men from the town went to look for him but couldn't find him. That night the *urcututos* (the owls), screamed. It was a bad omen and a sign of tragedy, as if they were telling us that Uncle Ramon had died.

He had been absent three days when his fate and location were revealed to my mother in a dream. She saw everything that had taken place through his challenge to the *Chullachaqui*. The next day she went to the place where there was a *cetico* tree that had roots growing out of the ground shaped like weapons, like rifle handles. Just as my mother had dreamed, my uncle was there embraced in the roots. His body was nearly only bones, because the vultures, ravens, and hens had been eating him. Although the whole area stank, my mother didn't smell anything at that moment. She was so overwhelmed with feelings for her brother, that she didn't mind embracing his rotting bones. Then she went back to fetch other people to help her bring his half-eaten body back for a wake that night before his burial.

What I learned from the story of my uncle's harsh fate is that even if one is an *ayahuasquero* or healer, one should not challenge any spirit. When we respect the spirits and ask for their help, they are here to help us, and they always come. The *Yacurunas,* the *Chullachaqui,* and other spirits from outer space come with powerful energy to heal any illness.

Chapter 5
Selling Pineapples in Iquitos

When I was thirteen and in the third grade, I fell in love with Irmita, the young daughter of the director of the school. In the evenings I'd stay out later than before, because I was always talking to her and kissing her, and hugging her. I didn't have a sexual intention, but simply the innocent love of a child.

My grandmother would give me ten *centavos* a day. With it I would buy two long English toffees with a green and white spiral pattern, the green part mint flavored and the white part anise flavored. Irmita and I would both suck them, then I'd give her mine to try. She'd take my candy with her teeth, and I'd do the same with her candy. After a while the two candies were not enough, and I didn't have any more *centavos*. So I told my grandmother, "Ten *centavos* isn't enough for me now, please give me twenty *centavos*." Our money system was made up of one, two, five, six, ten, and fifty copper *centavos* pieces and of bills called *soles*. You could buy a loaf of bread with one centavo or a larger loaf with two *centavos*.

"What? Twenty *centavos*? Work if you want twenty *centavos*! Instead I'll give you twenty lashes, you'll see!" she shouted at me. And in fact she arose at five in the morning and holding a wide belt that belonged to my grandfather, called, "Now why have you asked me for twenty *centavos*? Do you have a girlfriend? If you have a girlfriend, you're going to have to work to support her. She then hit me while I screamed.

All the neighbors heard my screams, and when I came out of the house they all said, "They beat you, they beat you!" I was ashamed that I'd been beaten and even more embarrassed that everybody knew about it.

From that time on, I started thinking of what I could do to make money. Then I had the idea that I would gather pineapples, and I looked around the school for the kids that were my age, to help me. I contracted lots of children to help me by carrying pineapples, and I paid them five *centavos* for each one. In Iquitos I could get fifty *centavos* for each pineapple.

I had a small boat and an oar that my grandfather had made especially for me. It was the one I always used when I went to the other side of the river to pick up vegetables and fruits from his land. Despite the fact that the Amazon was sometimes very rough and windy, nothing could stop me. Since I had learned not to be afraid of the Amazon River, during vacations when there was no school I'd go there almost every morning at dawn.

One evening, I filled my boat full of about a hundred pineapples. I'd promised the kids that had helped me five *centavos* for each pineapple they had carried from the field to the port at Tamshiyacu. From the boat I told them, "I'll pay you when I return from Iquitos."

My grandmother who was in charge of everything at home, asked me, "What are you doing with these pineapples?"

"I'm going to Iquitos to sell them, because you don't want to give me twenty *centavos*, and that's the way I'm going to earn my own money."

"But such a journey should only be made by grown men. The Amazon River is very wide and many people have been taken by the *Yacurunas*. You can't make the trip!" my grandmother said.

"Yes, I am going to Iquitos!" I replied.

I packed my woven bag, which was coated with rubber resin from one of the jungle trees. In those times there was no plastic, so we made our own bags. The men would sew the bags, hang them on a pole, and cover them with the milky resin from a certain tree. We'd cut the tree, and the resin would drip out all night into a pot, and by morning the pot would be full. Then using our hands we would cover the woven cotton bags with the resin, waterproofing them. I put my clothes, a blanket, and all the other things I'd need for the trip in my bag and tied it well so that if it was dropped in the river or if it rained, everything would remain dry.

My grandmother followed me to the harbor, in an attempt to prevent me from taking this first trip to Iquitos. Trying to pull the oar away from me, she pleaded with me, crying, "Don't go Agustin. The *Yacurunas* will steal you!"

But I was very strong, and my grandmother was old, so I triumphed, and grabbing my oar and pushing my canoe onto the river, I shouted, "Good-bye, grandmother! I'm leaving. I'm going to become a man."

There were, in fact, many stories about people who have disappeared while traveling whose boats have been found at the river's edge. Although large alligators or boas living in the marshes of the Amazon could have eaten the people, their families, to satisfy themselves, usually claimed that the *Yacurunas* had taken them.

By the time I left for Iquitos it was already 6:30 in the evening and the older men, who also traveled every evening, had already left. They had two or three hundred pineapples, while I only had a hundred pineapples in my boat, but it was completely filled. After shoving off, I began to row hard to catch up with the older men who were way ahead of me, but I couldn't catch up with them since they had a head start of more than a half-hour. I wanted some companionship so that I wouldn't have to travel alone, and I called after them into the night, but heard only the waters of the Amazon River. I had to journey across the Amazon alone.

The night was beautiful, with a moon and a sky full of stars. The Amazon was perfectly calm with no waves. Since the boat was very full even small waves could have capsized it, but I wasn't afraid. I took comfort in the sounds of the river, the lapping waters, like tiny drumbeats, and the mysterious sounds that came from its depths — sounds I couldn't identify but which might have been fishes or frogs. Once I saw a *palometa* fish, which looked like a plate, lying in the water and I pulled the fish into my boat. It was the most enormous fish I had ever seen, and I hit it so that it wouldn't jump back into the river again. The Amazon seemed full of life.

In the hope of meeting someone else on the river, every once in a while I called out, "Friend, friend" with the only response being the repetitive echo of my own voice, "Friend, friend....." bouncing off the river's edge. Once when I called out somebody did respond. I could barely make out another boat. I yelled, "Wait for me, wait for me!" The echo resonated. Then I rowed swiftly toward the voice. When I reached the place where the voice had been, there was nobody there. Although I could barely see, I continued traveling by the light of the moon.

Further on, midway between Iquitos and Tamshiyacu, I saw a luminous ball of light approaching, about thirty meters away. Then a great big red ball passed over me and my boat, illuminating everything in a red glow. It was like a huge ball of fire, which was extinguished at the banks of the Amazon, exploding in a display of many different colored lights. I didn't know what this mysterious phenomenon was but, unafraid, I continued on with the journey determined to reach my goal.

Further on, I heard the sound of a whistle. Then I became afraid because all children are taught that such a whistle is a spirit of someone dead. I began to pray "The Lord's Prayer" in a loud voice, which I had learned with the priests. This recitation strengthened me, and my fear dissolved.

I was getting closer to Iquitos when I saw a gigantic serpent approaching me across the waters, rising and lifting its enormous head. To get away from it, I rowed madly towards the beach and slept there until dawn. When I looked out to the middle of the river in the light of the day, I saw that what I had thought was a serpent the night before was actually a huge tree that had fallen into the river and had been wedged onto a sandbank. The flow of the river made it rise and fall like an undulating serpent, and two of its branches had the appearance of a large open mouth. I had also thought that the flow of the Amazon was bringing the object toward me, when in reality it was I who was moving toward the tree.

As a result of this experience I contemplated for a while how we often fear things that are not real, and what effect this has on our behavior and view of life.

I was now so close to Iquitos that I could hear dogs barking and the sounds of cars. At that time there were many cars in Iquitos which had been brought by foreigners. Iquitos was then a city full of English people, Italians, Chinese, and Spanish. There were many big stores with goods that had been shipped from Europe, and lots of commerce. At that time it was easier to study in Europe and England than in Lima. Access to Lima was more difficult. Because it was costly to travel, people who wanted to send their children to study in Europe would send them in ships from Iquitos. Everybody wore white suits and white hats, but the majority of people didn't wear shoes. Shoes were primarily worn only on festival days, on Christmas, New Year's, or July 28, the national holiday of Peru.

The buyers would come out into the harbor to meet farmers and assess their goods before they pulled into port. Soon a buyer arrived in an empty boat and asked me the price of my pineapples. I told him they were fifty *centavos* a piece. When he said fifty *centavos* was too high, I insisted on that price.

"You have to take them as they are, without choosing. One hundred pineapples, actually 105 pineapples to make up for any that may be damaged," I said. Finally he agreed and paid me. Since he saw that I was young, first he had tried to load the fruit in his boat. But I realized that he might be trying to cheat me and I said, "You have to pay me first before you can put the pineapples in your boat." Ultimately he paid me fifty *soles* in silver coins — a large amount of money and more than I had ever held in my hands!

Then with an empty boat I went on into Iquitos. There I left my boat at the port, where there were many houseboats, paying someone fifty *centavos* to guard it.

I went into the city without shoes, as I didn't have any. At the market I bought a large bag of bread, which was very inexpensive. I also purchased some checkered cloth for my grandmother so that she could make a long skirt like those worn by the old women, canned butter, and some ground coffee. For myself I bought a pair of shoes and two packs of Kool cigarettes to smoke when I returned. I was already smoking at that young age, although I never used to inhale the smoke into my lungs.

Later that night I returned to the port with all my purchases to sleep in my boat. At 2:00 in the morning I awoke, and left Iquitos for Tamshiyacu. On the way, at another port, I bought a breakfast of bread and coffee with milk for twenty *centavos*. Having breakfast at that hour, I felt strong. I was in general a very healthy, well-built boy. I didn't have parasites as many people did because my grandparents gave me *ojé*, an antidote consisting of the latex from a tree, the same cure for parasites that I now give to the groups that travel with me to my jungle camp, Yushintaita.

I continued my return journey, following the older, stronger men who were ahead of me, growing tired as I rowed endlessly. When I arrived at the first island that I had to pass, the sun was shining. At that point the sun started to become painful as I crossed to the other side of the river. Because of the heat I had to remove my shirt and my pants, and splash my body with water. My body was becoming dark brown, almost black, from the exposure to the sun. Occasionally I stopped under the shade of a tree, and ate the food that I had bought — soda pop, bread, a few tamales wrapped in cornhusks and filled with corn, rice, and meat. I drank water from the Amazon, which at that time was clean and uncontaminated. Nowadays, we can only use it to bathe in. We cannot drink it, although many people still do because they don't understand what pollution is. Later, to keep up my strength, I ate a little bit of *fariña* (toasted, ground *yuca*), adding sugar, lemon, and water from the river. This is then called *shibé*, and that enabled me to continue rowing. I ate this mixture out of the same type of gourd which is used to make *maracas* (rattles). When cut in half the gourd becomes a tumbler to drink water from, and this is called a *páte*. Despite the fact that the Amazon was turbulent that day, and I had to row very hard, I arrived in Tamshiyacu at 5:00 that evening.

I was happy to have had such an exciting and profitable adventure, which I related to my grandfather. My girlfriend loved

me more for bringing her biscuits and candies, and my grandmother was happy to receive bread, butter, and the cloth to make
a skirt.

As a result of this first successful trip, I made many other trips
to Iquitos during the two months of pineapple season. This is also
when the river begins to rise. After a week at school I would
journey there on Saturday, returning on Sunday. I continued con-
tracting the kids to help me carry pineapples to the port. Before
long they wanted to charge me more for the pineapples — six
centavos instead of five.

Each time I departed for Iquitos my grandmother still cried
and admonished me, "Be careful, the *Yacurunas* might take you."
Although the stories about *Yacurunas* were frightening, they were
also fascinating to me. I'd tell my grandmother, "If they take me,
I'll be happy."

The *brujos*, sorcerers, would call the spirits of those who had
been lost in the Amazon, acting as channels through which the
missing persons would speak so that the family could hear the
voices of the deceased, saying for example, "I am alive in an
underwater city where there are mermaids and men with fish tails.
There are great doctors, and life is beautiful and eternal."

It was said that the mermaids were lovely, with long flowing
blond hair and blue eyes. I would think to myself, "Oh, how I
would love to have such a woman — except for the fish tail." But,
then if you have been taken by a *Yacuruna*, you have already been
transformed into a man with a fish tail, so what does it matter?
According to local lore, during the festivities, the *Yacurunas*
emerge to dance, having been transformed back into very
handsome, enormous men and women. At the celebrations they
steal couples and take them to the depths of the Amazon, where
they live eternally.

My mother had told me that once she had seen a mermaid
dressed in a very unusual brilliant green, a color never seen on
this plane. At the time my mother was on the other side of the
Amazon, where my grandfather cultivated bananas and vegetables. She went to the harbor to get water, and amidst the sticks

and weeds on the shore, she saw the mermaid lying down combing her long, full blond tresses. She winked at my mother, who ran back to bring my grandfather to see the mermaid on the river bank. But by the time my grandfather arrived, the mermaid had disappeared.

By now I had become accustomed to traveling back and forth to Iquitos to sell pineapples. I was saving all the money I earned, and I would give it to my grandmother for safe-keeping. I was no longer dependent on her for money, but instead was able to give her some.

I had made about ten trips on the river, during which I had been able to feel the energy of the river, its spirits, its silence. Since there were no motorized boats on the river, I kept telling my grandfather, "Let's buy a motorboat, grandfather, so we can take all of our produce to sell in Iquitos."

But my grandfather would respond, "The best place for money is in the pocket. There you won't lose it." My aging grandparents had considerable wealth in fine silver, stored in the large trunks.

On my last trip to Iquitos, I encountered a ghostly ship, the same ship that has been painted by the well known artist, Pablo Amaringo. It is a phantom ship with lights, which appears on the river and from which are heard thudding sounds as if someone is making something with iron. On this occasion, I was rowing when suddenly little waves started to beat on my boat as if they were talking to me. I tried to row closer to the riverbank so that in case the boat overturned I would be able to swim ashore. Suddenly I saw the large phantom ship coming toward me and had to row out of its way to let it pass by. Then the ship started to sink into the water making a large whirlpool, about a hundred meters across, visible in the light of the moon. I was sure that if I were to go near the sinking ship, I would disappear with it. I escaped, and after the ship sank about forty meters from me, it passed beneath me, and reappeared further away continuing to float down the middle of the Amazon. I kept gazing after the ship until it disappeared, thinking, "That's the phantom ship of which my grandparents speak."

During my last return trip, after selling my pineapples, a river dolphin jumped into my boat. I had heard tales from fishermen that dolphins could be more sexually gratifying than women. There I was in the middle of the Amazon with a dolphin in my boat — a dolphin with small breasts and pubic hair just like a woman. I thought she had jumped into my boat because she wanted to have sex, so I took off my pants and had sex with her. Afterwards we both fell asleep. When I woke up, I realized I could have died being alone there with the dolphin for about two hours. Many men have died in sleep after having sex with a dolphin; it's important to have somebody there to hit you with a belt or a whip to wake you up. Luckily, I survived, and realizing it was getting dark and I had to get back to Tamshiyacu, I threw the dolphin in the river, and put on my black shirt and pants. The dolphin swam behind me in the water shrieking, "Je, je, je!" — as if she had fallen in love with me and was calling me. I escaped by rowing to the other side of the Amazon.

After that last trip, I felt that perhaps I was pressing my luck and that if I were to take another journey the *Yacurunas* might take me into the depths of the Amazon. So I did not go again.

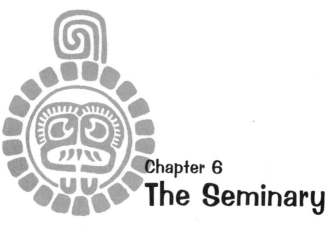

Chapter 6
The Seminary

When I was thirteen, my grandfather became concerned with my distraction of being in love with Irmita, and he decided it was time to speak to the priests. The outcome was that I was sent to the seminary in Iquitos to study for the priesthood. Only thirteen years old, I was very sad to go because I knew I would miss my girlfriend.

At the seminary I studied Castilian Spanish, Latin, mathematics, and theology. My mother and my grandmother would visit regularly, bringing chickens, pineapples, and bananas as gifts for the bishop.

Although I did well in my studies, I was very mischievous with a lot of energy and frequently upset the bishop with my behavior. I'd climb to the roof of the seminary, and from there I'd run around the rooftops, often playing together with a large monkey from a nearby institution who would come over to me. The bishop always disapproved.

One day there was a big storm with lots of rain that flooded the floor of the seminary. A radio was connected to one of the electrical outlets, and I was very inquisitive about what it was since we didn't have radio or electricity in Tamshiyacu. Out of curiosity I put my two fingers into the plug and almost died of electrical shock produced by water on the floor. Happily the electrical current only knocked me flying. The bishop, who happened to be looking at me at that moment, said, "This boy is crazy. He is a mischievous boy who apparently comes from hell!"

Because of the incident the bishop put me in a room with a skeleton and closed the door. He thought I would be afraid in there, but instead I enjoyed myself, touching and manipulating the bones. Watching me through a grille in the door, the bishop was astounded and said, "He doesn't have any fear, the foolish boy. He doesn't scream or cry. This is a phenomenon. Get out of there boy!"

After taking me out of the room, he then put me instead up on the roof of the seminary and took away the ladder. There was a ball on the roof from someone's street games, so I began to run and play with the ball, causing the roof to shake.

The bishop screamed to an aide, "Go and see what he is doing up there! The roof will fall in a minute! Take him down!"

Then he sent me to bed, which I didn't mind. I soon fell asleep. But then the bishop came and scolded me for sleeping, saying, "Hey, child, I didn't send you here to sleep!"

When I asked what else I should do in bed, the bishop said, "Get out of here! Go and take a bath!" But when I began enjoying myself in the bath, the bishop started shouting, "Boy, you will be there one hour taking a bath! What a naughty boy! You are not a good candidate for the priesthood. Go with your Bible to church to pray."

So I went to the church. After a while someone told me the bishop wanted to talk to me. Then he asked me why I had been in the church so long.

"The Bible was very interesting," I told him.

"What did you learn from the Bible?" he inquired.

"How to love," I answered.

"Oh, my! Go and eat lunch now," the bishop responded.

At lunch I sat near the bishop, who told me, "Sit in front of me. I want to look directly at you, so that I can see your horns." Nobody talked throughout the meal. I ate quickly, and the bishop once again reprimanded me, saying "Why are you eating so fast, child. Don't eat so fast you can choke."

The other seminarians were older than me but equally mischievous. There was a woman cook there, who had tremendous buttocks. One of them who was a priest always used to hit the cook's buttocks while she was cooking, which she liked. Because of behavior like this, I came to believe that priests are not very saintly.

Although I often misbehaved at the seminary, finally the bishop came to like me — no doubt for several reasons. I was the most intelligent of the seminarians, my mother brought food to the seminary on a regular basis, and I had found a wallet containing a lot of money that was never claimed. Eventually the seminary used the money to make many repairs and renovations.

I had found the wallet on my way to the market at 3:00 in the morning. It was full of 100 *soles* bills. It was rainy, and I saw the wallet lying in the street. Rushing back to the seminary with it, I banged on the bishop's bedroom door, yelling, "Monsignor! Monsignor!"

"What is it, child! You are crazy!" he said, not wanting to be disturbed so early. I told him that I had found a wallet.

The bishop had a scepter he gave me to shine every time I did something naughty. So he told me, "You will have to make my scepter shine like gold." He didn't want to get up, and so finally I pushed open the door of his room and turned on the light, and showed him the wallet.

"My God! Where did you find this, child?"

"In the street, Monsignor!"

"Poor person who lost this! Give it to me. Now go to the market quickly and try not to find another wallet."

So I went to the market carrying a stick and basket. I would always put the stick, with the basket hanging from it, in front of the butcher with money and a note saying how many kilos of meat the bishop wanted. The butcher would select the best meat. When I came out of the market I hung the meat on the back of a truck, and went to play marbles with some children. Then suddenly I saw that the truck was moving. It had gone two blocks away with my bag swinging from it. I started running very fast. After almost one kilometer, I finally managed to reach the truck and retrieve the meat. I now had to get back to the seminary, but I didn't have even one *centavo* in my pocket, so I held onto the side of a bus and traveled until the main square, where I got off. A policeman there had seen me hitching a ride and asked me why I hadn't paid the bus fare. I tried to explain, but the policeman didn't believe my story and asked me who my father was.

"José Rivas," I answered.

"Pepe Rivas?" he asked. People always knew my father by that name. "Pepe Rivas Varela, is he your father?"

"Yes, Sir."

"Pepe Rivas is my friend. I don't think he was as naughty as you are."

"Well I have to go back to the seminary, where I'm studying."

"Are you studying to be a priest? And you're hitching free rides on a bus! Go quickly or I'll take you to the police station and give you a spanking."

I ran back to the seminary, arriving there at almost 7:00. Everybody had already eaten breakfast, and the bishop asked, "Why are you here so late, Agustin?"

"Because I came back here to give you the wallet with money. Then when I returned to the market there were a lot of people waiting."

"Okay, I believe you," he said.

I was lying to him, so I had to confess this the next Sunday at confession. I considered what to confess and decided I'd have to tell about the meat. When I arrived at the confessional the priest told me I had to pray for contrition. Then he asked me, "What sins do you have, child? Maybe you have used the dogs or the hens to have sex."

"No, Father!"

"Have you had bad intentions looking at a woman, or have you masturbated thinking about a woman, child?"

"Yes, Father."

"That is a very big sin. You have to pray five Our Fathers, and five Ave Marias. What else have you done?"

"I lied to the bishop."

"My God! That is a big sin. How could you lie to the bishop."

I said. "At the market I hung his meat from a truck."

"That is not a sin!"

"But the truck left with the meat hanging."

"My God! So the monsignor was without meat, child?"

"No, Father."

"Then what is your lie? I think you will be lying to me after a while if you take so long."

"Father, the reason is that I ran after the truck, and I caught up with it very far away, and recovered the meat."

"But, where is the lie?"

"It happened on the way back to the seminary, the police caught me in the plaza."

"What happened with the police?"

"He asked me who I was and where I came from. I answered that I was from the seminary."

"How was that a lie?" continued the priest, getting increasingly frustrated.

"Well, when I came back, I told the bishop that I had arrived late because the line in the market was too long instead of telling him that I was playing marbles. That was the lie."

"But did you bring the meat to the seminary or not? If you did, then you did well. That is not a lie. But because you have taken so long to confess, you must pray twenty Our Fathers, and twenty Ava Marias." The priest admonished me.

As the priest was telling me to say the prayers in the confessional, I peeked through a hole to see who he was, because I had been many minutes, maybe a half an hour in that confessional.

That night I saw him talking to the bishop. I went up to them, and said, "Good evening Fathers."

The priest said, "Your voice seems very familiar to me. You are that naughty boy who confessed to me this morning for half an hour."

"He told me about the meat," said the priest.

"What about the meat?" asked the bishop. "He brought the meat here in the morning."

"I bought the meat, hung it on a truck, then played marbles. Suddenly the truck disappeared and I had to run for more than one kilometer to catch up with it and retrieve the meat. That's why I was so late getting back to the seminary."

"So you lied to me, child," said the bishop.

"But the father told me that it was not a lie when I made my confession, Monsignor."

"But you went on forever about the meat, the police, and so forth," said the priest.

"Well the thing is that I lied to the bishop," I said.

Then the bishop told me, "Go to the room where the skeleton is and pray forty Our Fathers, and forty Ava Marias."

Around this time, my mother came to see me at the seminary, and told me she was going to Lima to change her life, because it wasn't possible to live in Tamshiyacu anymore, where she felt that she was always carrying a heavy burden like a donkey. She had grown tired of my uncles, her brothers, who bothered her about the fact she had not married my worthless father and that he didn't take care of me. I started to cry, because my mother and I knew how much I would miss her — as well as the food she brought us.

After my mother went to Lima I started to do even more mischievous things in the seminary. Every Sunday all the seminarians went to town together to have fun, usually to swim and dance. We were supposed to go in together and return together. But I always went off on my own, and then everyone was punished as a result and not allowed to go again the next Sunday. The other seminarians became angry because my misconduct had led to their punishment, and they beat me. Consequently the bishop claimed that I was corrupting the rest of the boys, and finally expelled me from the seminary.

Chapter 7
Artistic Influences in Lima

After being expelled from the seminary, I returned to my home town of Tamshiyacu. I was now fourteen. I was much stronger, and had had my first sexual experience with another person, who was a very pretty prostitute my cousin had taken me to. When I returned to Tamshiyacu, I thought that now that I knew how to have sex, I would go back and have sex with my old girlfriend, Irma. But she had another boyfriend.

Being home again provoked a nostalgia in me for my mother, so I told my grandparents I wanted to visit her in Lima. I had enough money saved from the sales of fruits. My grandfather told me I could go with a professor, Pedro Navarro, who was also travelling there to visit his family.

Since after age fourteen children had to pay full rather than half fare, when we purchased our tickets I said I was thirteen years old, which was believable because I was short. So I saved half the price of the airfare.

This was the first time I had flown in an airplane. It was a plane with four engines, and the turbulent flight caused everyone to vomit. It was also cold in the cabin, since it was not pressurized as they are today, and there were holes in the windows. Because I was curious about the holes in the windows I put my fingers out through a hole, and the wind took control of my hand, so that I couldn't pull it in again. I started to scream, and other people shouted, "His hand, his hand!"

The stewardesses came to pull my hand in and take care of a resulting cut, admonishing me for putting my hand out the window and frightening the other passengers. "Why did you put your hand out the window?"

"Why is the hole there?" I said.

By the time we arrived in Lima, the pilots had already notified airport officials about the accident. After landing they asked me who my father was and who I came with.

"I'm with this professor," I answered.

The professor then explained how it had happened. Fortunately, I didn't have any bones fractured in my hand, only the skin had been broken.

Finally, we left the airport and went first to the home of the professor's family, where we left our bags, then to the place where my mother was living. We pulled the cord that sounded a bell inside the house, but nobody came out. Soon a neighbor appeared and told us that my mother had moved to Chosica, forty kilometers from Lima, and was living in a place called Artist's Home.

That night I slept in Pedro Navarro's house, and the next day we took a bus from Lima to Chosica, where we asked the bus driver to stop at Artist's Home. The first person I saw when I arrived was a tall, thin old man with very little hair.

"Good afternoon, sir," I said, as he came up to me smiling.

The professor said to the man, "He's looking for his mother, Doña Desideria."

"Who is he?" asked the old man.

"He's her son," answered the professor. The old man excitedly called my mother. She hadn't known we were coming, and when she saw me she cried with joy and said, "Is it really you, or is it a spirit?" It turned out that the man was my mother's new husband — I hadn't known that she'd gotten married.

Artist's Home was a very beautiful place, with lots of fresh air, where many artists from Lima came for the weekends. It had gardens, rooms, and a big water tank covered with a corrugated metal roof, from which my new stepfather, Don Pablo Vega obtained water for the garden. I stayed on with them helping out with work by watering the gardens and cleaning the artist's rooms. They gave me a bedroom in front of a river, which I could hear pounding the rocks as it flowed.

I was happy to be there, but when I saw that Don Pablo mistreated my mother — hitting her and making her cry, and frequently insulting her with cruel comments, calling her stupid and uncultured, and a derogatory term for Indian, *chuncha* — I didn't like it.

Angrily I would try to defend her, saying, "My mother is not a simpleton."

"Yes, she is," he'd yell.

Since I was only a boy and he was a strong man, I couldn't hit him. When he hit my mother she would just suffer through it, which was very upsetting to me. One day I decided I had to take some action. Having an idea of what electricity could do after I'd put my fingers in that outlet near a wet floor, I took two poles of electrical cord and put one pole on the metal roof and the other in the water tank. Next time Don Pablo took some water from the tank, he received a terrible shock and yelled, "Desideria, your son is a mischief maker, he has to leave here!"

Then my mother answered, "If that's the case, I'll go with him." But despite the big problem I'd created, we didn't leave at that time.

One day I was lying on my bed in my bedroom when I saw the beam starting to crack over my head. The house was built with a thin layer of wood covered with dirt. Since I liked to go up on the roof and jump around, I had weakened the roof. I jumped off my bed, and at that exact moment the roof fell down on my bed, with two points of the beam falling exactly where I had lain, and passing through it. I had come very close to death. My mother and stepfather were angry with me claiming it was my fault for playing on the roof. They rebuilt my room anyway.

The Rimac River, which flowed to Lima, ran behind the house. My stepfather planted tomatoes near it, and because I threw stones into the river, causing it to rise, he could never pick his tomatoes and complained about my escapades.

Every Sunday I'd go to the other side of the river, where there were mountains. I had discovered that on top of these mountains there was a white mineral, in the form of a fine white powder. I began to think about how to utilize it in a business and came up with the idea of selling it at carnivals. Taking the powder, I covered my whole body with it. It was a very brilliant white like the color of a pearl. Carrying a bag filled with about ten kilos of the white powder with me, I returned home painted with the powder and wearing a hat but no shirt. When I arrived, my stepfather started to run, calling to my mother, "Desideria, there's a demon here!"

My mother came and asked me what I had done. I responded "Mama, I've discovered this mineral, which I can sell at the carnivals."

"Ahh! Be careful, it could burn your face and your body," she said.

"I don't feel it burning me."

"Go and look in the mirror!" she said. Looking in the mirror I appeared like an extraterrestrial. Only my eyes and my teeth were white, while the rest of me was the color of shining pearl. Then my mother sent me to remove the powder in a bath, which was very difficult since it was greasy. After scrubbing myself with soap to no avail, I had to take a bath with kerosene. After that my whole body was red and it burned all night long. My stepfather said. "Now maybe you learned something!"

The next day I told my mother, "I'll make small paper cones and fill them with the powder, then tie them at the end, and sell them." I proceeded to make up five hundred, and sold them in the Plaza for twenty *centavos* each. It was my first business in Lima, and a great success; people really liked them because they were cheap to buy and good to throw at each other during carnival. Others bought cones from me, then dividing them into three packages, sold them. Soon people were asking me to supply them with more powder. So I went to the mountain again and brought back five big bags full. Some boys helped me carry the bags and make the cones. After a while I had the papers, with which I made the cones, printed with the name of my product, which I called "Silk Talc", because it was like silk and stuck to the body once it was on. Soon I sold more than one million of the little cones, making a lot of money, which I put in the bank.

One day my mother said to me, "Well son, now that you have a business and money in the bank, we can move to Lima." So we moved to a house in the Jiron Cusco in Lima, with a large interior garden, where the performing artists of Lima, and great Spanish bullfighters, like Juan Belmonte and Conchita Sintron, used to have parties. My stepfather looked after the garden and helped the artists when they came on the weekends. In those times, the artists would bring wine and food to their parties, and I would help by serving. After the parties, I'd gather all the bottles and sell them to a wine factory, which would pay me twenty *centavos* for each one. Still another way I made money was to pick the many varieties of flowers, including jasmine and roses, which we had in the garden, and prepare bunches of them to sell on Sundays at the central market. Because of these ventures I always had money.

Although my stepfather liked me, he wanted me to be serious, obedient, and respectful. Instead I was mischievous. The solution that both he and my mother agreed on was to see that I worked and didn't remain idle. So in addition to my own business enterprises, I also worked with my stepfather who was a hard-working man. He bought shirts, tools, and balls, and I'd sell them at the Parada in Lima, which was a major marketplace, and at the beach of Agua Dulce. Also on Sundays I'd sometimes sell used, top-brand shirts in the market, which my stepfather would buy from families after someone had died or from a consulate after someone had left for another place. After my mother had repaired, cleaned, and ironed them, I put them folded in a plastic bag so that you couldn't see where they'd been repaired and I'd sell them for five or six *soles*. In addition, I'd sell little chests with keys that my stepfather would make. I always had good luck with my sales at the market, which were profitable.

Next to us was a school for Japanese children. We would hear the noise of their playing in our garden, and their balls would land there as well. Soon there were about forty balls in our garden. The Japanese kids would yell, "My ball, where's my ball!" Although I wanted to return them, my stepfather did not. So every Sunday in the summer, I'd collect the balls in a bag, and go to the Agua Dulce beach to play with them. Then all the children would come up to me and ask if they were for sale. Very quickly all the balls were sold.

While at the beach I liked to jump into the ocean and swim. One day when I was jumping in, I fell down and twisted my ankle. I couldn't jump again for a long time, and even now it's sometimes painful.

Another activity I loved at the beach was watching men lift weights. Eventually I began to lift weights myself, developing my muscles. In addition, I liked observing people practice boxing there. After a while of watching others box, I decided to try it myself after a man asked for volunteers. My contender and I sized each other up, showing our muscles, and then really began the fight. The other person hit me first, and then I hit him back, straight to the heart, and knocked him out so he was almost dead and couldn't get up.

Then the organizers asked for another contender to fight me, saying "He's very tough. You have to be careful. He hits very hard. He's not from Lima, but from the jungle, a descendent of the Indians, and very dangerous!"

Finally someone else volunteered to fight me, saying to me, "I'll kill you!"

"You can try," I replied. "but you will feel the fury of my fists." Angry, he started jumping in front of me, and after preparing myself, I knocked him out.

"Are you a boxer?" the people asked me.

"No, it's my first time."

"If you can box so well your first time, think how good you might be as a professional," they said.

At that time I was very strong. I'd spent many hours rowing on the Amazon, which had made my wrists like iron, and I'd also been lifting weights, which had developed my muscles. All the girls admired my body, and when I was on the beach, they'd say, "See that rooster, how beautiful he is!"

My time in Lima had started to widen my horizons, giving me a larger perspective on life than the small village of Tamshiyacu possibly could.

Chapter 8
Going to Pucallpa

After spending almost a year with my mother in Lima, I returned to my grandparent's house in Tamshiyacu, where I stayed and worked for a short time. During that past year I had met my father for the first time. One day he came to Tamshiyacu to take me to live with him and my stepmother in Pucallpa. He was a mechanical engineer who managed a sawmill, made steel boats, and welded.

While living with my father in Pucallpa, I remember he bought me shoes and a pair of Champion brand pants, which wouldn't wear out because they were so thick it seemed like they were made of cow hide. It was the first time that my father had bought me anything, and I was almost fifteen years old.

My stepmother, Doña Imelda, would make me go to sleep at six in the evening because I had to wake up at three in the morning to get in line at the market to buy meat. At that early hour it was still dark, and I could hear the whistling of *difuntos*, or *tunchis*, as they call them there, spirits of the dead. It is also said that when a person is going to die, their spirit begins to whistle. These were the same sounds I had heard while traveling on the river. Although my body would shiver, I wasn't afraid. I'd continue on to the market and buy the meat.

After returning from the market, my stepmother would tell me to fetch water from the Ucayali River, which was about a hundred meters from the steel shop where we lived. It was my duty to fill two tanks of water every morning, each tank holding about sixty gallons. I enjoyed carrying water, and bathing while filling the tanks, but my stepmother was harsh in forcing me to do the hardest possible work. So one day I told her, "You make me carry too much water. I'm not a donkey." When she told my father what I had said, he threatened to send me back to my grandparents. I agreed he should. He immediately found me a boat and sent me off, simply because I had talked back to my stepmother. Then she didn't have anyone to carry water, so they sent for me again a month later.

I had been making trips to Iquitos to earn money, when my father came to fetch me in Tamshiyacu.

"Let's go," he said.

"No! I'm not going," I told him.

Then my uncle, who was a cousin of my father's brother, came to me with my aunt, Manuela Piñeiros. They said, "Agustin, come to Pucallpa, and you can live with us." I accepted the invitation. My grandparents were sad because I was leaving them again but I wanted to go where I could continue to learn new things. Also, I liked being close to my father, although I didn't like my stepmother.

From Tamshiyacu we first went to Iquitos, where my Aunt Manuela was chief nurse of the Santa Rosa Hospital. She had adopted an infant whose mother had died there, and they were bringing this child along, as well as my aunt's other son. In fact, the whole family was moving from Iquitos to Pucallpa, to work together with my father, who was employing my Uncle Reinerio.

We traveled the Amazon and the Ucayali River by night, in a steel tug made by my father and powered by a very powerful Caterpillar motor. Along the route we saw huge alligators six to eight meters long. At that time, around 1948, there were enormous alligators living on the edges of the river.

Awakening the next morning I went to the stern of the boat, where we had a bucket tied to a rope. I saw that the bucket was gone. My cousin, the eldest son of Aunt Manuela, had untied the rope and dipped the bucket into the river. Because he didn't let go, the force of the water-filled bucket had pulled my cousin into the river. I was the only one awake shortly after this happened. I could see him partly submerged, his hands waving in the air as the boat sped away. Luckily, he had not yet been eaten by an alligator.

I screamed, "Roger has fallen into the water!" since I thought it was the baby they had adopted. Everyone suddenly awoke. We brought the boat back and discovered it was my other cousin, who had fallen in. By that time I had jumped into the river to save him. They left me there swimming, picked up my cousin, and then returned for me, throwing me a rope so that I could get into the boat. I was afraid of the alligators, but fortunately the noise of the boat had kept them away. After the rescue operation, we all imagined with horror what could have happened if I hadn't spotted him or one of the aggressive alligators had been there.

We knew when animals from the jungle cross the river, the alligators have a feast, attacking like large sharks, catching an animal and dragging it to the shore to eat. Although the incident had frightened all of us, my cousin, Aunt Manuela, and Uncle Reinerio were very grateful to me since I had been instrumental in saving my cousin's life.

We continued the five-day trip to Pucallpa, traveling night and day. Every day I enjoyed new sights along the shores of the river, where a seemingly endless variety of plants grew, including violets, *jacarandas*, *huamansamanis* (a tree that has blue flowers), *aguajes* (palm trees with orange colored fruits), and the enormous *renaco* trees. Despite sometimes stormy weather, the boat was so strong and powerful it kept surging through the river. Because it had an electric motor, we had plenty of electricity, including an electric light.

As we approached more towns — Contamana, Tiruntan, Padre Marquez — on the last day before arriving in Pucallpa, we began seeing more boats and people. In those days there weren't that many boats and people. Now all along the Ucayali there are towns, houses, large boats, and slow moving boats called *peque-peques* with the standard engine of the Amazon which uses less fuel and has a characteristic thumping sound.

Eventually we arrived in Pucallpa, where my aunt and uncle had a house, because my uncle already had been working with my father. Soon after I had settled into my aunt and uncle's house, my stepmother came and asked me to live with her and my father, but

I refused since she had made me work so hard.

However while living with my aunt and uncle I also worked hard filling tanks with water, because we had to carry it from the river. At that time the Ucayali River was clear and unpolluted, and one could drink its water directly — nowadays one can't. I also split scrap wood I'd get from the sawmill with an axe. I worked hard because I liked it. I was strong because as a child my grandfather had always given me *ojé* to drink, a resin to eliminate parasites and enhance strength. Today I give *ojé* to my patients.

While living in Pucallpa, I started attending school, beginning with the fourth grade, since I had finished the third grade in Tamshiyacu. Although I was generally a very distracted student, I liked art. I'd make *huacos*, Inca-style pots with faces. I always got the highest grade in art because my creations so successfully imitated ancient pottery. I was also very good in mathematics, but I didn't like history because the history of Peru was so complicated — with stories about the Spanish conquest and various battles. Later I began to gain a better understanding.

My father had bought me a pair of very sturdy mining shoes with steel toes that were much envied by my fellow students who would step on them out of spite. One day when there was a torrential rain, I returned from school with my notebooks and books soaked. I put them out to dry by the fire, together with my mining shoes, which I put on top of the wood, since the fire was not too hot. Then I got distracted while getting more wood and having lunch, and it was only later I suddenly remembered my shoes. By then the shoes were burnt. When my father found out, he scolded me, saying, "How could you have let your shoes burn, stupid. You're a donkey." As a result I had to go to school without shoes because they wouldn't buy me another pair.

Later, determined to rectify the situation, I told my father, "I am going to work to buy myself shoes."

Because I was already inclined to carpentry I asked a nearby carpenter, Señor Soto, if I could help him, and he agreed. Since I lived next to the sawmill where my father worked, and where there were wooden planks of mahogany and cedar, it was easy for me to give him wood. But he said, "I don't want it free, I want you to sell it to me." So I'd look for good planks left behind by boats exporting wood to Lima or Iquitos, and I'd split some for our firewood and sell the rest to Señor Soto, who paid me two, three, and five *soles*. I saved the money for new shoes which would cost forty *soles*.

As another means of earning money, I also began to make hinges. At that time the only hinges there were left over from World War II, and I knew of no factories producing door or suitcase hinges. Because the sawmill had sheets of metal used for boats, as well as all kinds of tools, it was easy for me to make hinges. With mechanical scissors, I'd cut the steel, fashioning hinges everyone admired. I then sold them at a good price.

I also learned how to make wooden suitcases with metal corner pieces, which were commonly used in Iquitos at the time. I even made one for myself at Señor Soto's suggestion. In general this was a good period of my life. I liked working with wood and metals very much, and such craftsmanship awakened my imagination and creativity.

Ultimately I was able to save enough money to buy new shoes exactly like the ones my father had originally bought me.

I entered the fifth grade at age fifteen. I was younger than the other students who were mostly seventeen to eighteen. Since at that time education was not compulsory, children could be in the first and second grade at age ten to twelve, and start secondary school when they were seventeen. I went to a small school, with less than twenty-five students in my grade. During the term, the students fooled around a lot in the classroom. As a result I got bad grades, and our entire class did not advance to sixth grade. So I didn't continue my studies.

Another major change in my life around this time was that my father was imprisoned for making cocaine. The owner of the sawmill where he worked had started producing and marketing cocaine in Peru. As a mechanical engineer, my father built and serviced machines, and he had invented and built a machine to make the cocaine. One day the police arrived to investigate while my father was in Lima preparing a laboratory for cocaine. Since my father was not there, the police took me to the police station for fifteen days to interrogate me. At the time I didn't know what my father was doing, because he hadn't confided in me. However, eventually the police caught my father in the laboratory and arrested him with the other drug dealers.

Around age sixteen, Aunt Manuela who worked as chief nurse in a hospital in Pucallpa, got me a job there working on the generator that produced the electricity for lights. For a while, I devoted myself to learning about and maintaining the motor at the electric power plant.

Each day I tried to get my work with the motor done as quickly as possible, so I could help out in the hospital. I had a romantic interest in the young, pretty nurses, and I wanted to help them so they'd have sex with me. I'd blow kisses to the nurses nearby while I helped out by sweeping and mopping the floors, and bathing patients, many of whom couldn't stand up. In addition, when a patient died, sometimes the doctors asked me to help them when they were taken to the mortuary for an autopsy. I was happy to do this since I was fascinated to see how they cut up the body. With a saw and scissors, they would cut into the head, opening the skull, and then the sternum, so that the heart, the liver, and the intestines were exposed. Then the doctor would examine the body parts to determine the cause of death. For example if the liver was black, big and swollen, the person might have been poisoned or died of excessive alcohol, or if the heart was bloody, the person might have died of a heart attack. Watching the progression of the autopsy, I'd usually know what had happened before the doctor would give the results of his examination.

Once they brought in a Shipibo Indian woman who five days earlier had fallen into the water drunk, and drowned. She looked like a huge swollen balloon, and nobody wanted to carry her, not even her relatives, because she smelled so bad. So they had prisoners carry the woman to the mortuary in exchange for their freedom. The doctor and I entered the mortuary to see this enormous swollen corpse that stunk terribly. They made me put on a white gown and cut into the woman to begin the autopsy. As I cut, the stomach exploded, and even through my mouth bib I could smell the body's stench. Then quickly we noted the cause of death, and the doctor said, "The liver is black. She died of alcoholism. Let's sew her back up immediately." I grabbed the needle and sewed her shut and left as fast as I could.

I participated in numerous autopsies because I liked anatomy and I wanted to know about the body's interior. Today I see that having learned about the body this way has undoubtedly helped me understand the problems of ill people who come to me for healing. In the spiritual healing and operations that I do now, I can use the power of my thoughts with a precise knowledge of where the problems occur in the body. When I operate on somebody, I clearly recall the location of every organ, and am able to focus in very specifically.

If a person has a liver illness, I'm not only going to treat the liver, but the underlying problem as well, such as alcohol abuse or over-indulgence in hot spicy foods. Such problems begin in the stomach, then progress to the small intestine before the toxic substances end up in the liver. Thus, to operate on the liver, I need to understand the patient's behavior prior to the illness — what they ate, how they lived, and what kind of toxins they had in their body to cause liver problems. In my surgery, I cut into the liver in my imagination, because everything is imagination and thought in such surgeries. I enter the compromised organ with my mind, and if I don't know which organ is involved, then I do general surgery. In a general surgery, my wand will go automatically to the area where there is sickness. The wand's power involves giving off special rays to pierce the body like a laser. Even if the brain, the heart, or the eyes are fine, I need to pierce all those organs energetically. The surgery is done over the entire body. In many cases the results are positive, depending on the level of spiritual contact between the patient, the shaman, and others assisting in this ritual. That's when the miracle of a healing happens.

When operating mentally through our thoughts, the instruments we use can be anything — a wand, our hands, or even a knife — because the surgery is actually performed by the mind. When the mind is focused with intent, then one can allow the energies of the universe to work through one. In this way, healings occur.

Chapter 9
Mastery of Carpentry

After this period, I once again returned to Lima. My father's second wife together with their three daughters had moved there, and my brothers, from his first wife, were also living there. In Lima it wasn't possible to continue my studies, and my mother was concerned I wasn't learning a trade. I wasn't lazy and had always devised various ways of making money, but I hadn't developed a real trade. Meanwhile my mother was still suffering in her marriage to my abusive stepfather, who was very jealous and didn't appreciate all her work. About this time she was attending a school to learn sewing, and had started sewing items for sale.

While in Lima I regularly visited my Aunt Odisa, my father's sister who lived near the ocean in Magdalena del Mar with my step-brothers. There I'd eat, and help to cook, clean, and repair the house, but I always returned to sleep at my mother's house.

One day, knowing a sculptor was working in a studio across the street, I looked through a peephole in the door and saw him carving the figure of a woman in marble. I enjoyed watching the way he carved and eventually I fell asleep there. When the artist came out of his studio he saw me sleeping at his door and woke me to ask why I was there.

I answered. "Forgive me. While I was watching you carve the sculpture I fell asleep."

"So you're going to be an artist like me? When you want to, just come inside and watch me," he offered.

The next day I went again to watch him through the peephole. I was afraid that if I went inside I'd interfere with his work, that he'd feel he was being watched. I liked being alone and independent, and thought the artist could work better if he also had solitude. Although his work was very interesting, I once again fell asleep at his door. When the artist again came out of his studio and saw me, I explained that I had been watching him work. He said, "You're going to be a good artist, perhaps a great sculptor."

This remark filled me with joy, but I didn't tell the artist I wanted to work with him because I had seen that marble was difficult to work with. I was more inclined to work with wood.

One day at my aunt's house, my brother Ronald started criticizing my manner of speaking. I had a different accent, having been raised in a jungle town, while he had grown up in Lima. I was offended, so I slapped him in the mouth causing blood to drip from it.

Outraged, my aunt cried, "Look at this savage who has hit his brother!" and grabbing all the silverware from the table, she threw them at me. I ran for the door, and had already made my exit when the silverware crashed against it. Then my aunt yelled, "*Socarijo*, never come back here again!" as I ran down the road.

After that I didn't go back there again, until one day my brother Ronald and my other brother, (Coco) José, came to my house and said, "Agustin, *La Tita* (the name they called my aunt), says you can come back, all has been forgotten. I've also forgiven you for hitting me. It was just a small cut on my mouth. *La Tita* was upset because she saw blood." That day I had to go to work, but I told them I would come on Sunday.

Because my mother was worried that I wasn't working at a job where I could learn a skill, she went to talk to a cousin of mine who worked in a carpenter's shop that produced ladders, sawhorses, ironing boards, wardrobes, chests of drawers, and wooden trays. I liked the idea of working there, and after I spoke to the owner, he accepted me. I started out as a helper sweeping up the sawdust, boiling glue, and assisting when needed. Soon I got the idea of painting pictures on the wide wooden trays with decorated handles, which were used for carrying dishes or fruits.

My paintings were inspired by the dancers and bullfighters of

Lima. In the garden where we lived, dancers occasionally performed a typical Peruvian dance, called the *Marinera*, a dance of mixed heritage — part Spanish and part Negro. The women wore special long, colored dresses with shawls and adornments, while the men wore white pants and shirts as well as hats, and danced with a handkerchief in their hands. I also enjoyed watching the Lima bullfighters, or *matadors*. At the same time I began painting simple images of vases with flowers.

Although I enjoyed painting on the trays and thought about becoming a painter, I still preferred working with wood. One day when I was cutting wood with a machine, I became drowsy due to the summer heat and the constant drone of the machine, and cut off a piece of my finger and half the nail.

After that I couldn't work for a month. This break allowed me time to reflect on the work I was doing. Being intelligent, I'd learned very quickly how to make the ladders, ironing boards, wardrobes, trays, and other items produced at the shop, but I wasn't satisfied and wanted to learn more. The wooden trays always sold well because of my paintings, but I realized I wasn't doing very inspired work.

My mother had always wanted me to learn how to make fine-quality carved furniture, so she spoke to my stepfather. He worked in another furniture workshop that produced fine-quality carved furniture, in the style of Louis XV and XVI. After my stepfather spoke to the owner, he agreed to employ me.

There I worked, first as a helper, cleaning the large workshop, preparing glue for the furniture, and assisting the masters in polishing the furniture. At that time there was no prepared glue sold in cans; instead glue would come in small pieces like rubber, which had to be boiled in water, then poured through a filter into another pot sitting in hot water, and let stand overnight.

Although I didn't mind these tasks, because I'd already been working in another carpentry shop, I wanted to do more with the wood itself. I had already brought some tools to this new job, but I couldn't use them because I was required to do the menial tasks of a beginner.

In time, I advanced in my job. I was first assigned to sanding the small round tables and beautiful carved legs for the furniture. Then I became a master's assistant. Meanwhile I watched and learned how the masters, who liked my enthusiasm, handled the wood in the machines and created the carvings. I also bought myself a wide chisel, a curved chisel for the curves, and a large plane, so I then had a full set of tools. After many months of working at this shop and learning various skills, I decided it was time to leave and establish my own carpentry shop.

Before I set up a shop, I moved to a house that had previously belonged to a Japanese man. My stepmother lived there together with my step-sisters, Maria Rosa, Pelusa, and Teresa. My father was still in prison, where I would sometimes visit him. Seven people had been killed in that house. The previous Japanese owner had been accused of the crimes, but the real killers were members of the Dragon Sect, who trafficked in opium. The Dragon Sect had made the Japanese man take responsibility for the killings to avoid being murdered along with his family by the Sect. The police caught him when he was being forced to take the bodies of the victims to the river, since the Sect framed him by alerting the authorities. This Japanese man was taken to the same penitentiary as my father, who came to know him there. He told my father that he would die before he told the truth, because otheRwise they would kill his family. Consequently, he had offered his house to my father, for his wife and children to live in.

The part of the house where the people died had not been opened up for many years, and we lived in another section. However from an upper window I could see into the room where the seven people had died. There were still the footprints of hardened blood, and dust. It was a very large house with an orchard, and there were still automobiles which hadn't been moved for twenty years because the Japanese was in prison.

Since my stepmother and my sisters had no one to take care of them, I was like the father of the family. I now knew a lot about how to make cabinets and various other types of furniture, so I set up a workshop and began making wardrobes, beds, small, round tables, and chests of drawers for clients. Meanwhile my father also made guitars in prison, and friends of his would place orders for them at my workshop. To help my father's cause I made a gift for the Spanish ambassador, because my father was Spanish, and another gift for the wife of President Manuel Odria, Doña Maria Delgado de Odria. Although Doña Maria Delgado de Odria couldn't help my father, the ambassador of Spain was able to get my father freed. When my father obtained his freedom, he went to Bolivia.

After a year of operating my own workshop, I encountered a master who I had worked under in the carpentry shop. He was now working for another furniture factory that produced very artistic, carved and sculptured pieces. He offered me a job as general manager, which I accepted as I hadn't been getting much business on my own.

For two years, I worked there successfully. The workshop was like my home. I didn't do extra work on the side because I made seventy *soles* a day, which was enough to live well in Lima at that time.

With my salary, I also supported my mother, who then lived in Lima. By that time she had left her husband. She lived in a simple house where there was only one water pipe for many poor people, but she didn't want to leave because she had become accustomed to the place. She sewed high-quality clothes which were purchased by Jewish women although I basically supported the household.

Chapter 10

Che Guevara and
Social Consciousness

I met Che (Ernesto) Guevara in Lima when I was about eighteen years old. At that time he was known as Ernesto Guevara. Later he was known as Che Guevara, and became the renowned revolutionary leader who fought injustices for the peasants of Latin America. He joined forces with Fidel Castro, and fought in the Cuban Revolution as Castro's right-hand man. Later leading the guerilla fighters in Bolivia, he was captured by the Bolivian army in October 1967, and killed.

I was on the street when I encountered two men who asked me if I knew of a cheap hotel. I couldn't recommend one because the hotels around there were filthy and dangerous. They were foreigners and my interest was peaked, so we started a conversation. Ernesto Guevara told me they had left Argentina by motorcycle. After the motorcycle had broken down, they had hitch-hiked and finally arrived in Peru. They looked dirty and obviously had very little money, so I offered them a place to stay.

At my house my mother was very friendly, inviting them to eat and welcoming them as guests in our home. We were very poor and our house was extremely small, without running water or a drainage system. So when somebody needed to use the toilet we had to use a bucket, then take it to an alley, where we would dump the contents into a sewer pipe. Because the area was very poor, people went to this same area to a water pipe to wash themselves and the dishes. It smelled like shit, but that's how the people had to live. Ernesto Guevara could adapt to any condition, and stayed with my mother and I for about ten days. He and and his friend slept on an old mattress we placed on top of cardboard laid out on the wooden floorboards, and I slept up in the attic.

During their stay with us, Ernesto introduced me to his way of thinking and his insights into social problems, not only in Peru but all over Latin America. He made a tremendous impact on me at the time, and opened my mind to a view of the world I had not previously known about. I knew nothing about politics or socialism in those days.

While they were in Lima, Ernesto and his friend, went to meet Dr. Hugo Pesce, who was a well-known physician and a leader in leprosy research, as well as being a Marxist. Ernesto and his friend were both studying to be doctors, and shared his interest in leprosy and maleria, and other diseases which affected the poor. Dr. Pesce helped Ernesto, who was always dressed in dirty clothes that were almost rags by that time, by giving him a new suit of clothes and making arrangements for his and his friend's journey from Lima to Pucallpa, and then up the Ucayali and Amazon Rivers.

When Ernesto left, I asked him to write to me from wherever he was. I had come to feel a great friendship and admiration for this man. He did write to me from Pucallpa, where he stayed for several weeks helping doctors with medical treatments at the hospital, and also from Iquitos, and Manaos. He told me about his journey to many of the small and poor villages along the Amazon, and the conditions that he saw. He was interested in finding out if the people were educated, if the children were going to school, if they received medical assistance, and if they had enough work. In letters to me describing what he was witnessing and feeling, he said he found very poor people with eight, to ten, or sometimes fifteen children; alcoholic fathers; young women becoming prostitutes due to poor economic conditions; lack of electricity and sewage disposal, resulting in the increase of tuberculosis and other health hazards; wide-spread illiteracy among children; and poor hospitals and roads hampering effective treatment in emergency situations. Such realities made him very sad. I personally couldn't do anything about such conditions, and could only reflect on them after reading his letters.

By boat, Ernesto and his friend traveled to visit villages, where they gave consultations and treated patients with the medicines the hospital had given him.

When they stayed in Tamshiyacu for two days, many people in my town got to know Che Guevara. Although there was no hospital in Tamshiyacu, and unfortunately they were running out of medicine, they helped people the best they could, giving shots, as well as pills for asthma, parasites, and headaches.

Che Guevara's last letter to me was from Mexico. In this letter, he told me about his stay in Iquitos and travels beyond. In Iquitos he had picked up a large quantity of medicines from the hospital, as he had done studies along the Ucayali River on several illnesses, the same illnesses prevalent from Iquitos to the south. Everything had been done through his connections with Dr. Pesce.

Even before meeting Che Guevara, I already had an inclination to work with people which is why I'm still working for social causes today. At this time I am especially interested in working with children because they have a desire to learn, and they are the future generation.

Chapter 11
Lost in the Jungle

At age nineteen I returned to Tamshiyacu. One day I got lost in the jungle. I'd gone hunting, and completely lost my sense of orientation so I couldn't find my way back to the town. I went deeper and deeper into the Amazon jungle.

After sixteen days of wandering through the jungle, I ended up on a river full of alligators and boas. By constructing a raft out of some trees and pushing it along the river with a wooden pole, I managed to keep myself from being devoured. I remember hitting a huge alligator with my pole to frighten it off so it wouldn't attack me. Determined to survive, I ate raw birds and animals, since I didn't have anything with which to start a fire, only a rifle and a machete. At night I'd sleep in the trees because of the many jaguars in the area. Fortunately I had a strong will to live, which kept me alive.

Following nineteen days of survival living, I was exhausted and emaciated, with filthy and torn clothes. I wondered if this journey would ever end. Suddenly I heard people shouting. It was a group of Indians, bathing naked in the river. Leaving my rifle on the shore to avoid frightening them, I approached.

Surprised at seeing a man appear alone in the jungle, they surrounded me in a circle, holding up their bows and arrows. The spirits must have been protecting me. Strangely, one of them spoke a little Spanish, and I was able to make myself understood. They were a fierce tribe of Yagua Indians living deep in the jungle. They had no communication with civilization, except for the man who was my translator. He was the only tribesman who had been exposed to other cultures, having come originally from another tribe that lived closer to towns, which had been contacted by missionaries. He had come to live with the Yaguas to escape the encroaching civilized world. It was my good fortune that he happened to be with this group I encountered.

I told him I was from Tamshiyacu and was lost in the jungle. They said the village was very far away, and there was no one who could help me get back. Although their chief and the tribe didn't like strangers, they decided to take me with them.

There are different tribes of Yaguas. Some were more civilized and had started to cooperate with the timber companies who were exploiting the jungle resources. They were being used as workers. Other Yaguas lived much deeper in the jungle and had no contact with civilization. They were fierce warriors with customs different from those adopted by the ones who had abandoned their tribal ways.

That's why there are Yaguas in the Amazon. Some of them are in the universities too, working as bilingual teachers. Possibly the tribe that I was with made their way out little by little to civilization. I gave them a lot of teachings while I was with them.

When I was a young boy living in Tamshiyacu, we would occasionally see Indians who were coming from places deep inside the jungle where they lived in tribes. They would come completely naked, usually to get some rum. Today you cannot find such tribes, even if you walk for days in the remote regions of the Amazon jungle, although they may still exist in Brazil.

When we got to their encampment, they immediately locked me in a hut. I thought, "Maybe they want to kill me to prevent disease from spreading in the tribe." I was afraid because I knew they weren't partial to strangers, but I was also relieved to have finally stopped my wanderings through the jungle.

After a few days they allowed me out of the hut. Eating whatever food they offered me and drinking *masato*, fermented *yuca* beer, I began regaining a little of the weight I had lost. Then some of the young men challenged me to a fight, testing my strength. The *cacique*, the head man, watched me and could tell that I was a good man, strong, who wasn't afraid to fight. From then on, my presence in the tribe was more accepted. I was the first stranger from a non-tribal society to have ever come there.

One day, after I had been there a couple of weeks, the *cacique* sent me into the jungle to hunt with his son. The jungle there was very dense with vegetation, and contained many animals. It had not been destroyed like the jungle areas closer to towns. The Indians had a keen awareness of animal conservation and even raised species; including *piurís* (a black fowl as big as a turkey with a black crest, white breast, and long, red beak. Its meat is juicy and delicious), *pucacungas* (another type of bird), *trompeteros* (a jungle chicken), *majases* (nocturnal, huge, semi-amphibious rodents with gray hair spotted with white, and with incredibly delicious meat), *añujes* (one of the smallest rodents of the Peruvian jungle, but with the strength of two rabbits, and very delicious to eat), *sachavacas* (tapirs), and deer. Those animals raised to be eaten only at ceremonies and rituals were actually breastfed as babies, by women in the tribe who had milk in their breasts.

On our hunting trip I was following behind the *cacique*'s son when suddenly he started screaming and running. Thinking that he'd been bitten by a snake, I looked carefully ahead. I saw a human skeleton. Returning to the encampment, I found him vomiting foam from his mouth, with the other members of the tribe at a loss about what to do.

Since childhood I had known how to use tobacco smoke to heal because my grandparents, my uncle, and my mother were all healers, and I had been brought up in an environment of natural medicines. I knew I could dispel the man's fear of having seen the bones by blowing tobacco smoke on him. I asked for some tobacco and a pipe, and after I blew tobacco on him to cleanse him and protect him, the Indian recovered rapidly. I was grateful that I had learned how to heal with tobacco, instead of healing like the *brujos* who have to do such a long ritual for healing that a patient can die before they're finished.

There were about 200 people in the tribe. The majority were children because each man had from two to seven wives, some up to fifteen if he was capable of taking care of that many. When I first began living among the tribe, I stayed alone in a small house, eating on my own. Each family ate separately from the others, roasting their own meat after the men had hunted. They didn't store any food in their houses except plantains and *yuca*. When they wanted meat, they'd hunt in the jungle, and then immediately consume it. They went far from the encampment to hunt, thus maintaining the flora and fauna of their immediate surroundings. There wasn't a big variety of fruits, but there were ripe plantains, papayas, lemons, *aguajes*, and *pijuayos* (two types of palm fruit).

Time passed, and the Indians took me hunting with them, teaching me how to use a bow and arrow, or blow darts to capture animals, and how to climb up trees with ropes. Although I already knew how to do most of these things, I realized they were testing me so I practiced these skills with them to blend with the tribe. At the river, they kept their canoes, which they had made from tree trunks. Some of the canoes had also been stolen from other tribes. Nobody could go to have a friendly visit with those tribes, because of the wars that were caused through superstition and fear. We'd fish from the canoes and bring fish back to the tribe.

During the time I lived with the Yaguas I gained considerable knowledge and skills, and the spiritual aspects of my own life started to develop in a practical way. I came to appreciate the beauty of living so deeply in the jungle. It was also while I was with them that I began to use the curative powers and knowledge of healing learned from my grandfather and my mother, as well as the customs of the *brujos*, and healers, called *medicunas*, in Tamshiyacu. I started refining and using my past knowledge to help the Indians.

There were always illnesses in the tribe, mostly due to superstitious fears, promulgated by the *brujos*, who had power in that domain. The *brujos* would drink *ayahuasca* only so they could see what dangers were coming, what tribe was going to attack, or which other *brujo* from another tribe was sending bad sorcery.

Over the year that I lived with the tribe, I tried to help them understand they could live their lives based more on reality and less on superstition — ideas that I communicated through the man who had originally translated for me. I also introduced them to many new ways of curing illnesses, techniques which they hadn't known before. I, in turn, learned many ways of using plants from them.

I explained to them they did not have to be afraid of the *difuntos*, (spirits of the dead). All the people of the Amazon have a fear of the whistling of the *difuntos*. Usually when somebody hears the whistling of the *difuntos*, they crawl in bed and don't want to get out, and many people vomit. The only cure is to take a *shimitapon* (pipe), and blow smoke over them. As a result of introducing such new knowledge, and the fact that I had shown up suddenly and mysteriously in the jungle, the people began to consider me a god who had arrived to help them.

There was a treatment for labor pains already practiced by the tribe, and known by many people where I came from. It is the use of thin, dry sticks from trees, which are broken with a snap in front of a painful area. They release a gas that exists inside them, which eases the pain. This treatment also works for insect bites or even snakebites.

I showed the Indians how they could use clay on parts of their body to ease stomach, knee, or arm pain, as well as rheumatism. One wraps the clay in leaves, heats it on the fire, and then applies it to affected areas.

I was also able to show them a new method to enhance their ability to smell animals, the way dogs do, and also to increase their capacity to see in the night. For example, I'd learned from my grandparents how to mix tobacco with dry chili pepper and blow the smoke up another person's nose, releasing phlegm and improving the sense of smell. By contrast, the tribe's method for this was to grind seeds from a *pashaco* tree and inhale the powder. Mixing the *pashaco* seeds with *bubinsana* seeds, produced visions like *ayahuasca* does. Many of these strong *bubinsana* trees grew along the riverbanks, and we'd often grab their branches to prevent the river currents from carrying us away. After I introduced the alternative method, they found that the tobacco smoke mixed with *macusari* chili or *pucunuchu* was more effective, and allowed them to remain more alert for hunting since it didn't put them into a visionary state. It enabled them to be more skillful hunters.

For the purpose of creating ecstatic visions they also gathered toads that have poisonous milk in their bodies, and mixed this substance together with ground *pashaco* and *bubinsana* seeds. To prepare this mixture the poisonous toad milk was first dried and then ground up on a wooden plate together with the *bubinsana* and *pashaco* seeds, which had been toasted or dried in the sun, until a very fine substance was formed. Sniffing about one gram of this powder, they would enter into an ecstatic flight. It would also open up their noses to smell more clearly.

The Yaguas also had an ingenious way of strengthening the mouth to be able to blow a dart. For this purpose they used a hot pepper called *pucunuchu*. *Pucuna* means dart, and *uchu* is pepper in the Quechua language. They placed about five of these incredibly hot peppers inside each side of the mouth and kept them there all day long until their mouths were numb. This caused so much pain that they couldn't feel it anymore. Then when they blew the *pucuna*, or poisonous dart, they could do it with amazing strength, covering a distance of one hundred meters, stunning the animal such as a monkey, which they then killed by hitting it. The poison in the darts didn't kill the animals but only stunned them, allowing the Indians to catch and kill them. These people were also the best archers I have ever seen.

Fresh tobacco leaves were used to produce a snuff. Wrapping a piece of cloth made from *chambira* (a palm tree with spines whose leaves are used to make the fiber from which the cloth is woven) around their hands to prevent them from burning, they would rub a fresh tobacco leaf against a large ceramic plate which had been placed on the fire. This created a friction so that the leaf would give off a very fine powder that caused sneezing.

Fire was considered sacred, and was obtained when a lightning bolt struck a tree, starting a fire. They kept a fire burning constantly. If the fire were to die, there was no way of starting it again. But this never happened since fire was considered sacred, and was always maintained with thick dry logs constantly added.

Everybody had a fire going in their homes. If somebody's fire was dying, they would go to the home of another person and get a burning ember to get their own fire going. The fact that out of necessity they had to keep their fires going to survive left a deep impression on me. The common fire area was always swept clean by the women, using a plant like a long broom, called *sinchiqpich-ana*. They also made these brooms out of the *chambira* tree. After manufacturing their clothing from the *chambira*, leaf sticks were left. These were combined with *chambira* leaves and woven together and tied to make the brooms.

Another thing that had spiritual significance was eating human flesh. It was considered a special ritual to eat human flesh. They would not eat it to satisfy a physical need, but only for spiritual reasons — to be a warrior. Moreover they would only eat the flesh of brave people. Individuals who were cowardly in battle they would leave after killing them. They would only bring the bodies of the brave back from battles to eat. They believed that in consuming the flesh of a courageous warrior, they also received energy from his powerful spirit, thus enhancing their own ability to be strong warriors.

While the men would go far away into the jungle to hunt, the women would prepare the fire and the clay pots to cook the meat that the men would bring back. For good luck with hunting, we drank *ajosacha*, a jungle garlic. The *ajosacha* had to be small, with the root only as thick as a finger. The roots and leaves were ground up and put in water, and we drank and bathed in the resulting liquid.

Members of the tribe painted their faces with different colors for various occasions — such as births, deaths, marriages, cele-brations, or when the sun didn't shine and it was very dark.

These Yagua Indian women were very beautiful. They wove their clothing from the *punga* flower (a plant similar to cotton), or a very thin *chambira* (the palm tree). They wore a bib that covered their throats and part of their chests, without covering their breasts. They also wore little skirts, like a small apron, that just covered the pubic hair of the women and the girls. They never wore underwear, and many went naked. On festival days they painted themselves with the red dye of the *achiote* fruit. They didn't know about the different days of the week, only that when the full moon appeared it was the night to paint themselves. They believed that the light of the moon would give them youth and beauty. Living in the jungle, they generally didn't get sunburned. Their skin was neither white nor black but copper-colored. I encouraged them to sunbathe to strengthen their skin, because I believed that a certain amount of sun was needed to protect the body.

The tribe had a custom which prevented women from having overly developed or sagging breasts when they reached adulthood. Even old women always had pointy breasts. When girls were about six days old, using a clay spoon that had been heated until it was extremely hot, they would burn the baby's nipples. Afterwards they applied the juice from the leaves of the *ayrambo*, a plant with purple colored berries. If applied immediately to burns, it helps to prevent blistering. Later, when the girls matured, their breasts were small, although they produced a normal amount of milk when the girls became mothers, usually at about age fourteen. Girls married and gave birth as young as eleven or twelve.

The men wore longs skirts that went down to under their knees, or some went down to the ankles, but the men too often went naked.

Their blankets were made from bark of the *capinurí* tree, smashed and ground the way the Bora Indians make it. They used these blankets to protect themselves from the cold. They also had a fire burning under their hammocks. Because they didn't know about mosquito nets, they would burn termite's nests, called *comején*, to keep away mosquitoes. These nests were big balls, like huge houses where thousands and thousands of termites lived, and the fumes from the smoke would keep the mosquitoes at bay. At times when there were too many mosquitoes they would go into their houses, which had roofs made of leaves that went down almost to the ground. The doors and windows were made from those same leaves to prevent the mosquitoes and jaguars from entering.

One day I saw a very frightened Indian coming from the jungle, screaming that he had seen a spirit, the *Chullachaqui*. When the rest of the Indians saw him coming, they ran to their homes. Soon there was nobody to be seen in the encampment. I looked for the translator who was also scared and hiding out. I asked, "What happened?"

"He saw the *Chullachaqui*, and he's very dangerous. We can't go out when he has been seen in the jungle because he'll take us away and kill us!" answered the man.

"That can't be possible," I said, although at that time I was also a little scared and respectful of the *Chullachaqui*, considering my uncle's death.

Finally that night they all came out of their houses, and we sat around the fire. I told them, "The *Chullachaqui* is a jungle spirit and very good friend; he's not bad, and we shouldn't be afraid of him. I want to be a friend of the *Chullachaqui* so he can protect us and help us."

Gradually I also began to encounter the *Chullachaqui*, who would only look at me, then run away. He had a limp because he has only one foot. I wanted to talk to him, but I couldn't. Returning to the tribe, I'd say, happily, "Come, I found the *Chullachaqui*."

"Were you afraid?" they'd ask.

"No. I wanted to talk to him so that he'd be our friend. When we drink *ayahuasca*, we should ask him to participate in the ceremony. He's a powerful spirit that can give us whatever we ask for, so we shouldn't fear him but try to befriend him."

The translator would tell me, "The *Chullachaqui* is not going to come."

I would insist, "Let's try to bring him."

Then the *brujos* started to talk among themselves. They called the translator to ask him why I wanted to bring the *Chullachaqui* there.

I answered, "Tell the *brujos* what they know is not as powerful as what the *Chullachaqui* knows. He's a spirit, a god of the jungle; he protects the jungle and the animals. He can give us everything we want in the jungle. If we accept him as our friend, he'll help us win battles and have good hunting."

I used my healing abilities as much as possible to help the people. There were some old people who suffered from cold feet, especially at night. I'd blow tobacco smoke on their legs, massaging them at the same time. Instantly the cold would disappear.

A particular challenge was presented by a man in the tribe who for ten years had had a huge wound on his leg that wouldn't heal. According to the Indians, another tribe's sorcerer had bewitched him. Actually it was *uta*, white leprosy, which comes from the bite of a tick, or an arachnid, or a type of fly. This type of wound can spread over the entire body if a person's immune system is not strong enough to fight it. When I worked at the hospital in Pucallpa, I would give an injection of *repodral* or *wintro* to slowly heal the *uta*.

In an attempt to heal the man's wound, I washed the *uta* with tobacco, which the tribe had planted. First I cooked the tobacco and then washed the wound with the liquid. Then I chewed some tobacco, and covered the wound with the chewed tobacco. Afterwards I wrapped green *huito* leaves around it very tightly, picked from *huito* trees that grew by the riverbanks. In three months, the *uta* that the Indian had had for ten years was totally healed. The Indians and the *brujos* who had closely observed what I was doing were amazed.

After that everyone, including the *brujos*, asked me to help cure whatever sickness occurred. The people came to believe in my curing abilities and to regard me as another *brujo* in their tribe. I didn't allow them to involve me in their superstitions and fears. Because of this I think they were also able to relinquish some themselves. For example, they would invite me to drink *ayahuasca* then ask me if I could see if other tribes were going to attack us. I saw no attacks and no enemies, only friends.

As a result they decided to invite the other tribes to visit. To express this invitation they began to play the *manguare* (a percussion instrument made from a hollowed, dried log and struck with a beater), "tan, tan, ta, tan, ta, tan." Then perhaps thirty kilometers away we heard other tribes replying with the sound of their *manguares* telling us they were coming. The main reason for the gathering was to discuss medicine and various cures with other tribes.

One day I decided to put up a wooden cross in the encampment with a Christ-like figure on it. The Indians helped me make the cross, using a rope made of *tamishi* or *huambé* (a type of vine), to tie it up firmly. Then I found a tree trunk in the river that looked similar to a Christ, and we tied it to the cross. When they asked what the purpose of the cross was, I said, "This is to prevent anyone from attacking us." I was still very Catholic at that time, like my grandparents. Later my beliefs changed when I realized that the church often did more harm than good. I still regard myself as a Christian because I've been baptized in the Catholic Church and work with the spirit of Christ and the Apostles. God has given me many wonderful things in my life, for which I am grateful.

In the mornings I would go and look at the cross. When the Indians would look at it respectfully too, I'd ask them, "What do your feel? Do you feel anything special in your body?" Then I'd tell them they didn't have to kill the nearby tribes, that we could transform such energy through work.

So we began making wooden items, such as benches and chairs. Everything we made had to be tied together, because we didn't have hammers or nails. I created benches for all the families' individual patios and for the general patio, where they conducted ceremonies and competitive combat between youngsters.

Although I attempted to steer the tribe away from fear and superstition, these were a part of their nature and couldn't be entirely overcome. Even today the *ayahuasqueros* are supestitious, in contrast to my work which is not based on superstitions.

For the most part the tribe continued their traditions. They continued to have battles with other tribes and practice cannibalism. When the *brujos* said do something, then everyone in the tribe would do it. In that sense the *cacique* didn't have a say. So if the *brujos* said that a tribe was going to attack us, then we had to go and prevent them from killing us. When the *brujos* said we had to fight, the warriors would prepare, the *cacique* would get his lance with many shrunken heads on it, and we'd go to battle with our enemies. Before the men went to fight, they were not allowed to even smell a woman, and they cleansed themselves with a plant infusion.

Then with everyone painted, we would leave in silence. I was invited to go with them, and would always walk next to the *cacique*. Since I was considered part of the tribe, I had a duty to fight with them. Because of superstition they thought I had special powers.

If the moon was out, we'd leave when the moon was shining, making guttural sounds if we needed to communicate, as though we were birds or animals. When the *chiqua* (a bird that announces good or bad luck) sang, then we would go in a different direction.

When we arrived at the other tribe's encampment, although they might be quiet and perhaps have no intention of attacking us, we'd nevertheless get ready to attack. Forming a semicircle and all shouting together in one voice, we'd charge. They'd be caught by surprise with no time to prepare, and so would be killed. We wouldn't kill the women, only the men — sometimes unjustly because they hadn't planned an attack on us. I felt much sadness about the killing involved in such battles, but the *brujos* claimed it was necessary for our survival. I had to go along with what the tribe did.

During one battle I took my first trophy, the warrior who fought against me. He was strong with long hair. I remember fighting fiercely for almost an hour before I succeeded in killing him. I had to stick my lance across his neck, tearing up the skin, then grabbing his head and pulling it out from his body, with brutal force. I was so tired that he almost overpowered me.

Men who didn't have enough wives had to take women from a conquered tribe, as symbols of triumph. One purpose of such battles was to debilitate other tribes that represented a threat. The dead cowards, the ones who had died right away without a fight, were not picked up to be eaten. Only the warriors were. Then we would return triumphantly to our encampment. We took the body of the man I had killed, cutting it up and leaving the viscera behind. I took the head, left arm, and heart. The *cacique* carried the right arm, showing with gestures his thankfulness and admiration for me because I had revealed my bravery that night. They considered me a great warrior because according to them, I had killed the *cacique* of the other tribe, possibly Ticuna — a man of thirty or thirty-five, with fine features.

That night everything seemed to reflect my own sadness; it threatened to rain, and the moon hid among the clouds. We disturbed the *choshnas* and *musmuquis* (nocturnal monkeys), and the owls. We celebrated the victory because our tribe had left behind more than fifteen dead people. We had left the old women behind but brought the young women with us. The women knew they had to accept being assimilated into the conquering tribe. All the captured women were put in a separate house, like a jail, to observe their attitude towards us. If they behaved fiercely and were rebellious, then they would be killed since the tribe wouldn't keep women who refused to be assimilated. Even though the tribe had a predominance of women, they continued to steal women from other tribes because they wanted to try new women, and they considered it a challenge. For the Indians, the important aspects of a conquest were acquiring women, killing warriors to eat them, and shrinking heads.

By sunrise the next morning we were back in our encampment, where the women were waiting anxiously to know who had died. Only two of our men had been killed, and we had carried them back to honor them and burn them, and then drink their ground-up bones in the *masato*, a type of beer that is prepared with *yuca*, jungle potatoes, and the *pijuayo* fruit. In this way their spirits were liberated and incorporated into the bodies of everyone in the tribe. In the tribe it wasn't permitted to see a person rotting in a state of putrefaction; bodies were disposed of through burning. The bodies of the warriors they had killed would be lightly roasted in the fire, cooked just enough so the meat was bloody. They were eaten by everyone who had fought. They would eat most of the body, including the heart, the hands, the eyes, and the brain, but not the liver. The women and children did not participate in this ritual.

Just as it was the tribe's custom to go to war when the *brujos* saw sinister signs after drinking *ayahuasca*, so would the two *brujos* talk with the *cacique* about killing any man within the tribe who they saw as bad. They might decide that a man was bad if he wasn't functioning well within the tribal system, or was weak and couldn't fight, or had character flaws, or performed misdeeds. If somebody had insulted or abused another person, or raped or disrespected a young girl, they would be held accountable and would be burned alive. Nobody could even look at a girl that was passing by naked. You had to keep your head down. When a man wanted to have a woman, they first had to pass tests. For this reason, fights were arranged among the young men, who also had to be able to catch arrows shot at them and break them against their legs.

The tribe had a law, similar to that of the Incas, whereby a person was put to death for being a thief, a liar, or lazy, although it was acceptable to steal women from other tribes. This was considered a sign of bravery. Prolonged illness was also not tolerated. If a person could not recover in a reasonable time, they were burned or abandoned far away in the jungle to be eaten by the wild animals. Children who were born with deformities were burned alive in a very hot fire made with dry leaves so that it would consume them immediately. These practices were the way the tribe assured that only the fittest survived. They couldn't afford to take care of individuals who were not able to contribute fully to the community.

The Incas also had practices we would consider barbaric today. Many people were killed by the Incas, who would drink the blood of those killed and sprinkle it around during ceremonies. Many offered their lives to be sacrificed during potentially catastrophic events such as earthquakes or eclipses of the sun. Their deaths were considered ways they worshiped the sun god.

In addition the Incas had severe punishments, such as burying people in a hole and covering them with a stone, or hanging them. The Incas also killed by tying a stone around a person's neck with a leather rope and throwing them into an abyss. The head, with the stone, would separate from the body, and the vultures would eat the flesh.

When there were people in the Yagua tribe who were disagreeable to the *cacique* or the *brujos*, the *brujos* would drink *ayahuasca* to have a pretext to execute these people. In such situations, the *brujos* would say, "This man is bad, he should not be here," or "This man's a traitor," or "This man is lazy," or "This man is a thief, he should not be in the tribe." Then these men were invited to drink *ayahuasca*, and were given a very strong dose so that they would lose consciousness and could be taken to where there were *otorongos* (jaguars), or lagoons filled with alligators, or boas. There they would be eaten by animals without being conscious of it or feeling pain because they were inebriated with *ayahuasca*, which is called "rope of death, rope of justice, rope that elevates us, rope that gives us knowledge of the universe, or umbilical rope that represents the birth or rebirth of a person." According to the belief of the tribe, once such an individual had been devoured by the wild animals, he was liberated. His spirit could then be among them without causing fear.

When the tribe ate their warrior enemies, they would save the heads, without the eyes and brains, shrink the heads, and keep them as trophies. They taught me this process over the course of several days. First we cut the head in a certain way, then removed all the bones. Next we prepared a boiled liquid concoction made from the *pashaco* tree, which is very astringent and is also good for curing leather. We cooled the liquid, then put the head into it for two days. The astringency of the *pashaco* prevents the hair from falling out and the head from giving off a bad odor. After the skin and hair hardened, we sewed up the head like a bag, including the mouth and eyes which we sewed shut, with thread made from the *chambira* tree, and put wooden plugs into the nose and ear holes. Next we heated white sand from the river on a large ceramic plate on the fire, until it was burning hot, and filled the head with it.

The head had orifices everywhere from which it could be hung with *chambira* ropes. While we ceremonially shrunk the heads, we would drink *masato* beer prepared with bones of the deceased and eat the flesh of the dead.

We let the head sit overnight, and as the sand cooled down the head started to shrink and become hard. In two days, using the thin stick of an arrow, we removed the sand which was very compressed because the head had shrunk. Then we again put the head into the same *pashaco* liquid, repeating this process four or five times. Each time we soaked the head it would shrink again, until it became the size of a fist with long hairs. The facial features didn't change, but simply became smaller. The mouth and eyes remained sewn up, and only the plugs from the ears and nose were removed, since they were used again for other heads.

Such heads were like jewels or relics for the Indians. It was the greatest most powerful object one could have. The men carried them on the principal arrows, which were made from a palm tree called *huacrapona*, or from *pihuayo* or *aguajillo* trees.

The *cacique*, who had seven beautifully reduced heads on his lance, would tell stories about them that illustrated his bravery. He would say, "I fought for three hours with a very strong warrior to obtain this head. He gave me much energy and strengthened me as a warrior, to lead my tribe and wage war, although I follow the commands of the *brujos*."

Although I had participated in their rituals of killing and taking trophy heads, at the same time I was disturbed by such practices and attempted to get them to reassess the need for such activities. I beseeched them not to have *ayahuasca* ceremonies for the purpose of preparing for battle, saying, "We should not be having *ayahuasca* ceremonies only to go into combat or kill. Let us have ceremonies for seeing things that are positive and divine, for learning how to heal."

The people we had attacked had had no opportunity to prepare for battle, and had no intentions of attacking us. I questioned why we had to attack a tribe that lived two days away and that had not been giving us any problems. At the same time, I knew if the *brujos* said that we had to attack but some of us refused to go, then the tribe would have considered us cowards and killed us. Actions were dictated by the *brujos* just as governments are run by ministers, with the president only signing bills.

So they wouldn't realize I was trying to influence them, I gradually and subtly introduced the tribe to ideas about our civilization, including concepts of God and good spirits. They only knew about bad spirits and superstition. At times, all the tribes-people would gather and ask me about our culture, while the translator would translate.

If a plane flew over the encampment, I'd explain that they were machines with many people traveling in them. I would tell them about the very big cities that existed elsewhere, where they would have difficulty living because they weren't born there and were not educated in a school, and because they didn't speak Spanish. I told them many people outside of the jungle didn't like Indians. Then I would tell them what I didn't like was for them to live in savagery and to kill people because the *brujos* said that they had to. Further I would say I had only participated because otherwise they would have killed me. During the year I was with them, I managed to change their thinking about the practice of killing, influencing them with my civilized thinking.

I knew about a plant called *huayusa* that always keeps one strong and alert, without feeling lazy, weak, sleepy or hungry. After drinking it, you wake feeling energetic at three or four in the morning, and in spite of having a lot of sex, a man still feels strong. When I told some of the Indians about it, they all wanted to know about the *huayusa* plant and how to use it. I told them *huayusa* is first dried for eight days with wood smoke over the fire, then cooked and drunk — about half a liter of the liquid per person.

One morning at about four, after they had gathered and prepared *huayusa*, everybody drank the liquid. At the time there also happened to be a jaguar, the king of the jungle, nearby roaring. The Indians were afraid of the jaguar and didn't want to go out of the encampment.

"Today we will not go into the jungle. The jaguar will eat us. It's dangerous," they said. But I answered, "We have to go to the jungle because we need to pick some more *huayusa*. Because we just drank some, now it is necessary to go immediately so we can use the energy we have received from the plant."

So we went into the jungle, where the jaguar was roaring even louder. I encouraged them, saying, "Let's go! We cannot be afraid of an animal; we are warriors and have no fear. We have to walk through the jungle when the sun is coming up, because we have drunk *huayusa*, and this is the way we leave our weakness behind." Ultimately, the *huayusa* gave them the strength to complete the task.

In our encampment there were always sick children and adults with swollen bellies, caused by drinking unboiled water filled with parasites. I remembered my mother giving me *ojé* as an antidote. I knew what *ojé* looked like and had seen the *ojé* trees when we went down to the river to fish with bows and arrows. I realized I needed to teach the tribe how to use this plant to combat parasites. They had another remedy for parasites, which was effective but very dangerous, called *boliche*, or *huayllete*. *Huayllete* has a black seed inside, which they used to make necklaces, while the outer part, which produces a foam but is very caustic, was utilized like a soap to wash clothes. The peel was used as an antidote for parasites.

I told them about the *ojé*, and six men, including the *cacique*, went to collect it. Once we had located some trees, I taught them how to make cuts on the bark to extract resin from the tree, allowing it to drip into a ceramic container.

After we had collected enough resin, early the next morning people with the biggest bellies gathered to drink the *ojé*. I also drank it to give an example to them. They shit a lot, excreting about three hundred or four hundred worms, like serpents. One woman with an enormous belly expelled what looked like about a thousand worms. The *brujos* and the *cacique* also drank *ojé* and discharged hundreds of worms. As a result the *cacique* and the ill people were all delighted with the treatment and were happy I had arrived at their encampment to save their lives since, in the past, many children had died because of parasites. Many in the tribe had died due to lack of oxygen. Since worms go into the lungs, the liver, the kidneys, the intestines, the stomach, the larynx and pharynx, then come out through the nose or mouth, people can become asphyxiated, when they do not use remedies for parasites.

Another treatment I introduced to them was for stomach problems. For this I prepared pure tobacco liquid, not the way I make the medicine today, which is a highly concentrated mix of tobacco, coffee, and sugar. This pure tobacco mixture induced vomiting and cured the ailments. Later we discovered a leaf called *huancahuisacha*, a well-known means of inducing vomiting. After grinding it up, I cooked it together with the tobacco, and this mixture produced intense vomiting. This treatment, together with the *ojé*, helped heal many people of the tribe.

Also I introduced *chiriqsanango* to them, a means of treating colds and chills. *Chiriq* means cold, and *sanango* is that which heals the nerves, the cold in the nerves. They were always chilled or catching colds because they lived the majority of the time in the shade of the jungle with hardly any exposure to the sun, and sometimes it would rain a lot.

One day I saw three very sick, limping men with swollen ankles and pain in their shoulders, wrists, and elbows. I immediately recognized it was rheumatism, but they, with their superstitions, believed *brujos* from other tribes were hurting them through witchcraft. I tried to persuade them the causes were from the environment, telling them, "It's not from other tribes. This is a problem related to water, cold, humidity, and too much shade. You're not getting enough sun." Then I encouraged the men to expose themselves to more sun and told them I had seen *chiriqsanango* heal this problem.

"Okay, heal us," they said.

Then I advised them, "You can't eat meat, fruit, or drink *masato* for a month while using *chiriqsanango*. Eat nothing except plantains."

They agreed to this regimen, so one morning I gave them *chiriqsanango*. First I scraped the roots with a well-sharpened wooden tool, then gave three roots to each person being treated. As soon as they had drunk the *chiriqsanango*, they had to go to the water, because it's a strong plant that produces a burning like fire in the stomach and intestines. They felt very weakened and had hallucinations where they saw snakes coming close to them, wanting to insert their tongues into their mouths. I told them not to open their mouths, because if they did they would receive the worst energy of the medicine, that it was not good to receive the snake's poison, which would make them become vengeful *brujos*.

As the days went by, I made sure they were not eating meat, only plantains and water. Gradually they began to walk easier, get rid of the rheumatism, and a month later they were healed. They were very happy, and I felt the love they expressed. I told them to go and bathe rapidly, then to go into the sun and give reverence and thanks to it since the sun is our powerful father who gives us heat and health. Later five or six more people wanted to diet and be treated with the plant.

While I was with the tribe I learned a considerable amount about their craftsmanship. Some days when it rained a lot we'd make darts and *pucunas*, the long hollow tubes used to blow little poisoned arrows. The poison, called *curare*, was made from a poisonous vine called *ampihuasca*, to which we would add the hot peppers called *macusari*, spiders, and tarantulas, and then stir it in clay pots until it was the consistency of honey. Eventually it was applied to the points of the darts.

The best artisans taught this skill, and the knowledge of different arrowheads, to others who knew less. There were different arrowheads for various uses. The ones made for hunting birds were like balls, with no points. Others for big animals were wide so they would penetrate the skin into the heart, and the animal would bleed to death as the Indians chased after it, following the smell. The elders of the tribe passed on their knowledge about how to wage war, how to kill and how to make crafts, arrows, and poison for the arrows.

I also learned many of their cultural beliefs. They believed that when the owl, the *urcututo*, sang, it was a warning. As a result when this occurred at night, they'd go to their beds and not leave them the whole next day. They thought if they went into the jungle after such a warning, a snake could bite them, or they might be attacked by some animal.

Similarly, when it was the dark of the moon, they would refrain from work and sex that day. They believed that children conceived at such times might be born weak and sick. During a full moon it was considered advantageous to have sex as much as possible until the women became pregnant. Their idea of contraception was to take a pregnant woman to the jungle and scare her by telling her that the *Chullachaqui* was there. Then the men would run away, and the woman would be so scared to be alone there that she would start running and start bleeding, and lose the baby.

I also learned about their music, a very strange, mournful type of music created by playing flutes. At that time I also played the flute and drums, having learned these skills from my grandfather. However their flutes differed from those I was accustomed to in that they had no holes. So I made my own flute and was able to produce the sounds I wanted. The tribe had drums made from the skins of jaguars, river otters, or *sajinos* (wild boars). Their drums produced very good sounds and we would spend the night playing drums and flutes. I taught them how to sing and dance Peruvian music, coastal music, the *changanaqui*, the *citaraqui*, and the *pandillas*, which are dances from the Amazon. Such music was played in towns along the Amazon when there were festivals. The *changanaqui* dance consisted of a man and a woman dancing together, and as they raised their knees trying to hit each other on the buttocks with their knees. The fun of this dance was trying to avoid being hit on the buttocks. The tribe liked this dance very much.

I also learned some dances from them. They would dance naked for hours which was very erotic. We'd paint ourselves with colorful clays and dyes from *achiote* fruits which give a red color, or *mishquipanga* fruits that gives a bluish color. Usually we used red and white clay and drew stripes on our bodies so we looked like zebras.

Ceremonial dances were considered very sacred, but were also performed to entertain and to awaken sexual energy. The men tied their penises up to their waists with a rope, to avoid having erections. Since the penises were tied, it was dangerous for the men to have erections because their penises would turn black with the lack of blood circulation. Since both the men and women danced together, the men had to be careful to not think sexual thoughts as they danced up against the buttocks of the person in front of them. If men had an erection, they had to stop dancing until they lost their erection, loosening the rope until the flow of blood was normal.

The lines of dancers looked beautiful, like a big serpent. The *brujos* danced at the front of the lines, wearing feather crowns as a symbol of their status, and the *cacique* danced behind them. The *cacique* was well respected by the whole tribe despite the fact that he had an ugly face; when he smiled, only half of his face moved because the other side had atrophied, after his face had been cut deeply and one eye removed. This facial disfiguration had been done purposely as part of his initiation ceremony when he had become the chief.

Another common activity during the rainy season was hunting big toads, called *hualos*, which croaked loudly in the marshy areas of the jungle. We'd collect them in *shicras* (bags) made of *chambira*. It was difficult because these toads were agile, and it was hard to catch them. We'd spend the whole night following them, their eyes shining brightly in the darkness, until each man caught five or six toads.

Back at the encampment, we'd put them into big pots so they

couldn't escape. Even though we apparently killed them first, some of them would somehow come back to life — a very strange occurrence. The head of the toad had been almost cut off, and yet the next day it was back in place. The next morning, we'd skin them, then put four or five toads onto a bamboo skewer, called a *carrizo*, and roast them over the fire. The white meat was delicious, as well as the juice that came from the toads which was like a broth. The bones were soft like cartilage, making a crackling sound as we ate them. Eating them was a ritual with everyone sitting in silence and thinking of the toad they were going to eat. Toads were sacred animals to the tribe, animals associated with life-giving rain.

Another ritualistic food was snakes. Days were set aside for a group of fifteen to twenty young men, led by the *cacique*, to gather them. With a stick we'd move aside the foliage and dry leaves to look for the snakes, and when we found any, we'd jam a forked stick over their heads to trap them. Sometimes we'd find s*hushupis* (bushmasters), and *jergones* (fierce and poisonous snakes), the two kinds that were the most delicious to eat. The tribe wouldn't eat boas, however, because they were sacred. Like alligators, boas existed to serve the tribe by devouring undesirable people who had committed misdeeds. After catching the poisonous snakes, we'd take *aguaje* fruit from a palm tree, and holding the snake behind it's head, we'd make it bite into the *aguaje*, to release its poison. Then we'd cut off its head with a special sharp wooden arrow, which was similar to a knife. We'd only take the snake's body back with us, skinning it at the encampment.

At a meal, snake was always accompanied with *masato*. The women prepared *masato* by chewing the *yuca*, the saliva creating the fermentation required for this drink.

The Indians filed their teeth with special stones, until they were really sharp, and very dangerous. I tried to sharpen my teeth, but my body trembled with the friction from the stone, and I couldn't endure it. Luckily it wasn't mandatory.

The longer I stayed with the tribe, the more the *cacique* grew to love and trust me, believing I had been sent to his tribe for a purpose. One day the translator said, "The *cacique* loves you dearly, you're a strong man, and you're single. So the *cacique* is giving you his daughters. You need women here, so you won't look at the other men's women. He wants to see you at his home."

I went to see the *cacique*, who offered me his five daughters, all about thirteen, fourteen, or fifteen years old. He showed me their various mothers, and asked me if I liked them. Almost twenty now, I was happy to have five women. I liked these pretty women, especially their little pointy breasts.

The *cacique* explained, "These five women are only for you, but you cannot have more than five, and you cannot look at any other women." The women admired me and were happy I was going to be their husband.

The manner in which I had acquired wives was actually uncharacteristic of the tribe's usual process of mate selection. Generally men in the tribe who wanted a young woman, had to ask the permission of the *cacique* and pass tests of strength, one of which was killing a *huangana* (wild boar). *Huanganas* were raised by the tribe specifically to be sacrificed for this purpose. The *huangana*, had to be killed by an arrow directly into the heart. Men who could hit the heart were allowed to pick the unmarried girls they wanted and could select the number of women in proportion to the number of *huanganas* they had killed. The old women cut the dead *huanganas* into pieces with wooden tools and then divided the meat for ritual consumption.

Soon the tribe began preparing a huge feast to celebrate my marriage, inviting other tribes to participate. To announce the feast, every day they would beat the *manguaré* (hollow trees), that could be heard for a long distance in the jungle if the winds were favorable. We heard other tribes answering from as many as ten or twenty kilometers away, signifying they knew it would be a celebration.

For the occasion, they made plenty of *masato*, which they prepared in basins carved from *huacrapona* trees by hitting them with primitive stones tools. They would first hit these palm trees at their thickest part with the stones, then using their hands and the sharp edge of sticks, they would carve the center out like a small canoe, where they would put the *masato* to ferment.

On the day of the celebration, groups of twenty to thirty men, women, and children started to arrive from various tribes, the old people staying behind to take care of things. Everybody brought drums and flutes, as well as *masato* in a dough-like form, without the water added, which we put in large containers. Soon the encampment was full with people whispering, "The *cacique*'s daughters are marrying a white warrior, a God who came from outer space."

The young women that were to marry had to undergo ritual circumcision, in which the clitoris is removed, a ritual that is performed in almost every jungle tribe, including the Shipibos, the Campas, the Boras, the Candoshis, the Shapras, and the Ticunas. The ritual was performed after the women danced all night and had, along with the rest of the people, drunk enough of the strong *masato* beer to become intoxicated. After they had fallen to the ground inebriated, the old women of the tribe carried them over to a separate area, placed them over wooden boards painted white with clay, and ritually circumcised them with a wooden tool made from a *paca* plant, a bamboo-like plant, which had been sharpened in the form of a bird's beak. In such a state of inebriation from the *masato*, the young girls could not feel much.

Afterwards there was another ceremony of "deflowering" the young women. For this ritual they had a ceramic object shaped like an erect penis, which they heated up and inserted into the young women's vaginas. After that, to prevent bleeding, the women slept all day, while the celebration continued.

I thought these rituals were a terrible practice.

The marriage celebration continued for an entire month. To count the thirty days of the celebration, they used red, blue, or yellow feathers of the *guacamayo* bird for each day that passed. When thirty feathers had been collected, it signified the celebration was over.

After the celebration had ended, I still wasn't allowed to live with my women, although we could play and talk together. The translator told me I had to wait ninety days, again counted by feathers, to have sex with my wives. During that time the women continued to sleep at the *cacique*'s home.

After eighty days had passed, I began approaching my wives at the river when they went to get water. We couldn't understand each other, but I asked the translator to tell them they were beautiful and that we would soon be together since there were only a few feathers left.

Finally, after ninety days, the *cacique* told me his daughters were now my wives.

After that my women would wait for me at the entrance to the tribe's encampment when I would go out hunting, but it was not customary in the tribe to show affection by touching each other. Only at night would I embrace them to have sex — which was not romantic since it was not the custom for people having sex to excite each other through kissing and embracing.

When I had lived with the tribe about a year, I realized I could no longer stay with them since I missed my former life. I knew I had to leave and I also knew I couldn't take my wives with me, or let anyone know I was going.

So early one morning I gathered my bow, arrows, *pucuna* (a bamboo tube to put my arrows in), and told my wives I was going into the jungle to hunt. Then I left, never to return. By then I knew a way to the Amazon, because we had travelled once in that direction to visit another tribe with whom we were not at war.

I ran all day so nobody could catch up with me. For food I killed partridges with my bow as I ran, sucking their blood and eating their meat raw.

In the evening, I approached the encampment of the other tribe. Without passing too close because of the dogs, I circumvented it and was eventually able to connect again with the path. I continued walking rapidly all through the night and the next day, finally arriving at another tribe that was totally civilized. Here I didn't have to be afraid of being seen because the tribe I had been living with would not come that far. After travelling two days and a night, I had made it to the Amazon.

When I told the civilized tribe where I had come from, they said, "That tribe is fierce, and they're cannibals."

Finally, I jumped on a passing boat with my bows, arrows, and jungle clothing and went to talk to the captain, telling him the story of how I had been lost in the jungle for a year. After I asked for his help, he gave me clothes and shoes, and then took me all the way to Iquitos.

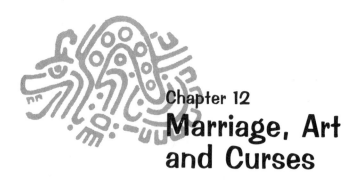

Chapter 12
Marriage, Art and Curses

After my experience with the Yaguas in the jungle, I went back to Lima and began making furniture again. Then for a while I went back to Pucallpa, where I met Dr. Teodoro Vinder, who had come to work in the Albert Schweitzer Hospital, which had been founded in 1942.

Working with him, I learned alternative methods of healing difficult wounds that would have resulted in amputation at other hospitals. For example, we'd cut the skin and wash the wounds with boiled warm water and *permanganato*. Then without gloves, using only our nails and fingers, we'd scrape inside the wound to cure people whose ankles were the size of a soccer ball with the bone rotting inside. We also cured tetanus and other kinds of infections in similar ways.

For three years I lived between Lima and Pucallpa, then traveled back to Iquitos.

There in 1955 I married a woman named Elena, but we didn't have children. Although she was a good woman and I was in love with her at the time, she was too jealous and possessive. She didn't want me to talk with friends because she thought we were talking about other women, and would only let me dance with older women at parties since she did not want any competition. One night I danced with a young woman despite her insistence, and Elena rushed home and wanted to kill herself. When I went back to the house, the door was locked, but I got in and went to bed. Then she hit me on the mouth, and I hit her back, causing her to scream. There was another party going on across the street, and when the people heard her screaming, they shouted, "Kill that bitch!" Everybody in the neighborhood knew Elena made me suffer. She probably behaved so possessively because she loved me so much, but other people didn't like her to treat me that way because they liked me in Iquitos.

After eleven months of living together, I told her I was leaving. Since I had built her a house in those months, at first she didn't believe that I was leaving her. I took my things to my uncle's house, and while I was bathing in the river, she got my belongings and took them back to her place. She said she didn't want to separate from me and promised she wouldn't be jealous anymore. I told her I had already set a date for the separation and I wouldn't change my mind.

Two years later, in 1957 I married another woman, named Soronjita, who was sixteen years old, while I was twenty five. My courtship of her the proceeding year was very romantic. Soronjita's father, Cesar Gonzalez, was an old, rigid man who didn't want me to marry his daughter. So we dated for a year without having sex, just hanging out in the street, hugging each other.

During that time, Soronjita worked in a medical clinic. Elena kept chasing me and saying I was still living with her so that Soronjita wouldn't want me.

Around carnival time I had some money and started to promote Soronjita for carnival queen. She won because I had put a lot of money into promoting her. I also bought her crown, scepter, and dress. Because Soronjita knew I'd helped her, we became closer friends.

Meanwhile, Elena was creating problems for me with Soronjita's father. He thought that his daughter and I were having sex, which was untrue. He didn't want Soronjita to marry me under any circumstances because he thought that I was also still living with Elena. The situation became worse when a *brujo* told Soronjita's father I was having sex with his daughter and the old man wanted to kill me with his rifle. I went after the *brujo* who had told the lie and fought with him. He pulled out a knife, and I kicked it into the river, somehow fracturing his arm. They took me to the police who learned that he had been lying about me and Soronjita. But they also told me I had to pay a pension to him for six months because he couldn't work with his arm in a cast.

I had a friend, an old man named Don Roque Rengifo, who'd act as a messenger bringing news between Soronjita's father and me. He once told me, "He's a dangerous man, and he doesn't want you to marry his daughter, and he still believes you are living with Elena." I begged him to tell Soronjita's father it wasn't true. Roque said the old man wouldn't believe him and that Soronjita was under age, only fifteen, so I couldn't do anything about the situation. Finally, Roque went to see Soronjita's father to tell him I had struggled enough for his daughter and had now given up hope. Then her father relayed a message for me to visit him. I was afraid he might kill me, but Roque said he was reconsidering the situation.

When I went there, Soronjita's father addressed me sternly, "Good day. I see that things cannot be solved otherwise and that Soronjita is very much in love with you. I have called for you to ask if you want to marry her."

"Yes Señor, I want to marry your daughter." Then he asked his daughter if she wanted to marry me, and she replied, "Yes, Papa." As a result, Soronjita's father gave his permission for us to be married. But since he didn't want to be involved with the marriage, he said he wanted to appoint an attorney to handle everything. In fact, he didn't show up for the ceremony or the reception. We were married by the bishop in church and also had a civil ceremony, followed by a big party with lots of chickens and beer.

After the party we went home, to a house I had built for us, and had sex for the first time. She was young and still a virgin, and people downstairs were listening to the bed creaking and Soronjita shouting. I had boiling water in a pan upstairs, so I poured hot water down on the floor, causing the people to scream and run away. Later, Soronjita got pregnant and in 1958 our daughter Odisa was born.

Around 1958, at the beginning of my marriage, I would go to

the jungle to hunt for food. In that jungle there weren't mosquitoes but there were many flies. If you were injured, the flies would get under the mosquito net, lay their eggs on the wound, and the maggots that would hatch out almost immediately, could kill a person.

On one hunting trip, I set up my mosquito net, dyed brown with mahogany bark, so it was camouflaged and animals couldn't distinguish it from the surroundings. As night fell I got inside it. It was a clear, moonless night, the sky filled with stars but still dark; perfect conditions to wait for animals. I had a good flashlight, a rifle, and a well-sharpened dagger.

Suddenly, I heard an *otorongo* (jaguar) roar, very close by, and my body trembled. I had a partridge hanging from the grill, that I'd killed earlier, and I think that the partridge smell attracted the jaguar. The jungle was otherwise silent, with not even the sound of a bird, and even the insects quieted down. The jaguar is the king of the jungle in the Amazon, like the lion in Africa. After a period of silence the jaguar roared again, about a hundred meters away. I was holding my rifle, with my flashlight in my left hand, and I thought that the jaguar was going to the watering hole to wait for animals, but it moved closer and closer towards my grill. Then I heard a little branch cracking on the ground. When I focused my flashlight on the spot, from three meters away there was an enormous jaguar weighing much more than a hundred kilos, looking at me with his mouth open, showing me his teeth. His tail was moving, and he was ready to jump. Back then I had lost my ability to smell animals, and I'd only realized that the jaguar was there because of the noise. My mosquito net was open, and my rifle barrel was pointing at the jaguar. With my hands shaking, I shot and the jaguar jumped. Then I threw myself to the ground, dropping the rifle in order to have my hands free to protect myself. It was totally dark, and I couldn't see the rifle anywhere, since the flashlight was off. Fearing that the jaguar was close and alive, I began to run into the jungle, crashing against trees until I saw one that was uprooted. I rushed into it between two roots; although my body and legs were still sticking out, and I thought that the jaguar would eat them.

After a while, when the jaguar didn't come, I thought maybe I'd shot him. Still, I waited many hours until morning. When dawn arrived, I crept out of my hiding place, which was difficult. In the process I scratched my ears on the roots of the tree, causing them to bleed.

When I arrived at my camp, I discovered that my grill had been knocked down, my mosquito net rolled up almost like a banner, and my rifle and bullets were scattered on the ground. I picked up my dagger and loaded the rifle. Feeling brave with the dagger and rifle in my hands, I followed a trail of blood I found. About twenty meters away, I found the enormous jaguar dead; the bullet had gone into its eye and had blown its brain out. I found that the jaguar had human hair stuck in it's teeth, undoubtedly from eating some Indian, so it could have eaten me, too. I skinned him, and also took his front and back paws, leaving his head with the body.

Then I began my return trip, carrying the forty-kilo jaguar skin tied up with a rope, along with a turtle that weighed about five kilos. Walking back the way I'd come, I began to smell gunpowder and realized that another rifle I'd left in a trap had gone off. As I approached the trap, I saw a huge deer that weighed about fifty kilos, lying dead. Soon I was carrying almost a hundred kilos back with me.

Carrying the load, like people do here in the Amazon, with a rope across my forehead and the load on my back, it took me four or five hours to get home. Later when I cut the deer open, I discovered she had a small fawn in her womb, which is why she had weighed so much. I sold some of the meat, and smoked and dried the rest for our own use.

Around 1959, our family decided to move to Tamshiyacu. At the time Odisa was still little, but Soronjita was already pregnant with our second child. I had an aunt who was an alcoholic but a good midwife, and she helped Soronjita during the birth of our second child, a daughter named Tete. I prepared numerous bottles of a medicinal drink of *ruda* with rum, to give to Soronjita to prevent her from having any problems after the birth. Since my aunt was an alcoholic, when she saw the medicinal drink she was very happy and drank a bottle every time she came to wash diapers. When the drink was gone, I filled the bottles with water, and she even then commented that the liquid was watery and tasteless.

It is customary when a baby is born to invite people to celebrate and drink the *ishpa*, which is a specially prepared liquor that we make for the occasion. This is named after the baby's urine, which is also called *ishpa*.

At this time I made money for the family expenses in a number of ways. First, I made guitars for sale. Constructing two guitars a week, I'd sell each one for 100 *soles*. I also worked as an electrician, installing lights. In addition I hunted in the jungle for meat and fished in the Amazon River, catching lots of fish, mostly *boqui-chicos*, which we cut, salted, and sun-dried. With the fish and the meat from the jungle, we were able to live very well, and have extra to sell.

In 1960 we moved to Pucallpa with our two daughters. This same year our son, Cesar Agustin was born in Pucallpa, and in the two years following we had two more children, Xiomara Adela and the last, Mirma Desideria, who unfortunately died.

In Pucallpa I established a small furniture workshop in an old house I fixed up. There I made various types of furniture, focusing on cheap beds, mostly cots for poor people. At that time beds cost a hundred *soles*, which was very little money, so anybody could afford them. To make them I'd buy pieces of scrap wood from the bigger workshops. Because business was very slow I consulted with a gypsy, Madame Carlota, who wore a long skirt, strangely decorated blouse, lots of gold and silver bracelets, large earrings, and a colored scarf wrapped around her head. She told me, "You have a curse on you and therefore no luck in your business." Then she offered to heal me and enhance my business if I gave her a beautiful kidney-shaped table made out of cedar, along with three pretty little benches.

She said, "I'll heal you. I've healed others who now have big businesses. If you give me the table and the three little benches, I'll heal you. But first you need to have the desire to be healed and no doubts of the healing's success. The table and benches should also be a gift from your heart."

After considering this proposal, I answered, "Okay, it will be my pleasure. I'll give the table and the benches to you, if you'll heal me."

A group of little kids was following the gypsy, as is usually the case with gypsies because they look so exotic. The kids carried the table and benches to her big tent, where she did divinations, palm readings, and card readings.

Then she told me, "Take some soil from your workshop, and bring a bottle of water to my tent." My workshop had a dirt rather than a cement floor. I filled up a bag with soil and got a bottle of water, believing fully in what she was going to do for me.

She went ahead to her tent, very happy with the table and the benches. By the time I arrived, she had already put my table in the center.

Next she instructed me, "Put the soil and the bottle of water on the table and sit down; we're going to work with you now."

Emptying the water into a tall glass, she covered it with a red cloth and prayed in her own language. As she uttered her magical words, the water in the glass started to boil.

"Look," she said, "this is proof of the curse. When there is no curse, the water doesn't get hot. Now we're going to pour the water back into the bottle again." I poured the burning hot water into the bottle and closed it with a cork.

Then she emptied the bag of soil onto a sheet of newspaper and prayed again. The soil didn't change color or become hot. It appeared normal. "All right, now do as I say. When you leave here, take this soil and sprinkle it all over the floor of your workshop. After seven days, sweep it up, together with your garbage, and dump it all into the Ucayali River. Put the bottle of water on the roof of your house for three days and three nights, uncovered. Let the sun, the moonlight, and rain, fall onto it. Nobody should see it. After three days you should bathe with the water at dawn. After bathing, walk around the block clockwise, without greeting anyone. In three more days it will be time to sweep the floor, get the soil and the garbage and throw it into the river. After this you'll be healed."

After this meeting with Madame Carlota, I returned home feeling happy, believing the outcome would be very positive. I prepared a place on the roof for the water, which I protected from cats that might prowl during the night.

After the three days had passed, I forgot to bathe with the water at dawn. When I went to Madame Carlota's tent and told her about my omission, she said, "Well, it's even better to bathe with the water tomorrow at daybreak."

The next morning at dawn I retrieved the bottle and bathed with the water. I did the other things she had said were necessary, including throwing the soil together with the sawdust from my floor, into the river.

Miraculously, three days later an engineer showed up at my workshop to order some work from me; his employees were building a highway from Pucallpa to San Alejandro, a river in the direction of Lima. He said, "I want living room, dining room and bedroom sets. How much will this furniture be?"

"I'll give you an estimate tomorrow," I answered.

When he returned the next day, I quoted him a price of fourteen thousand *soles*, the first contract I had ever made for that amount. It was a lot of pieces for me to make, but not a lot of money for him.

"How much do you need in advance?" he asked.

"Seven thousand *soles*, 50 percent."

"Okay," he said, never even asking for a receipt.

Later this man, whose name was Jaime Luna Trelles, became my daughter Odisa's godfather. I told him it would take a month to make the furniture. Although I usually used scrap wood, for this job I also bought some wood and other materials. I worked night and day like a titan. Exactly thirty days later I had everything ready. He paid me, and I put my money in a savings cooperative.

A few days later, another engineer showed up, wanting exactly the same kind of furniture. I told him that it would cost eighteen thousand *soles*, as I had made too little with the previous order, for the work I had done. Also I told him that it would take forty days, because I was exhausted from working so hard for the last order. He gave me half the money in advance, and together with the money I had made from the previous job, I had a good amount in savings. As a result my wife was happy, no longer suffering for lack of money, and my children had toys and could eat good food. I was grateful to the gypsy for her help and I wanted to give her a gift, but she was back in Lima.

In forty days, I had the furniture ready, which was beautiful. Soronjita had helped me weave seats made of Chinese straw for it.

As soon as I finished this job, the engineer's boss showed up, and wanted a cabinet made of one solid piece of mahogany four meters long and very wide, with door and dividers. It was to store silverware, plates, and cups.

"Sir," I said, "this will cost twenty thousand *soles*."

"Very well, but I want it really well done and of pure mahogany," he answered, seemingly unconcerned about the price.

He gave me a check for ten thousand *soles*, and I finished the cabinet in twenty-five days. Because the wood was one inch thick, it was very heavy, so that eight men had to carry it to the truck.

Shortly thereafter, he came back and told me he wanted me to make an extremely fine piece of furniture, in a special kind of wood cut in a certain way so that the knots were visible. Although the piece of furniture was to be small, I told the man that because it was a very fine piece needing special wood, it would also cost twenty thousand *soles*. He accepted my estimate without even questioning the price, and gave me half the money in advance. As a result, I had to ask the timber companies to get me this kind of wood with knots, which they did. They cut the boards for me, but they were very difficult to polish smoothly without little holes appearing — so then I needed special polishing brushes to prevent this from happening. Ultimately I finished the piece beautifully.

Because of all the furniture orders, I had started living much better, and there was no doubt that my luck had changed. So I rented some land with a small house in the center of town, in the same place where I still have my house in Pucallpa today. I fixed the roof so it wouldn't leak, and moved in with my wife and children. There we were able to live simply but well.

To improve productivity in my business, I bought a table saw to cut wood, so that I could do different types of work. Because the sawmills were throwing out large quantities of wood, my only cost for it was the price of transporting it by truck. I picked up the wood, and with my saw, made three or four beds per day, and sold them at a hundred *soles* each.

After a year of operating efficiently in this way, I began to make quite a bit of money and I had more that forty thousand *soles* in savings. In addition I could easily get loans when necessary because of my work.

One day I was making wooden beaters used for whipping up cooked ripe plantains, called *chapo*. This was a very successful product for me because of the lack of electric blenders. I was pushing a piece of wood through the saw when it spit the wood out, and my hand almost slid into the saw. Luckily I didn't cut off my hand, but I dislocated the index finger and broke a finger bone on my right hand. I saw about twelve bone doctors, but none could put the finger back in place, and there was sinovial fluid damage so that even today I cannot straighten my finger. After this accident, since I couldn't continue making furniture effectively, I decided to change my line of work.

Soronjita and I then established a juice business, making various juices in the market. At that time, nobody else sold juices, so our business was very successful because the many people at the market wanted to drink them. We'd get up at 2:00 in the morning and go to the market to open the stand; from 4:00 A.M. on, people would come from the river to buy goods. We made good orange, grapefruit or mixed juices, naming our business "The Vitamin Juice Bar of Mirma Gonzalez de Rivas". Our sign, with a nice painting of fruit, was made by a painter friend. I also got children selling the juices, paying them 20 percent of what they sold. We'd all take glasses filled with juice on a tray down to the port and sell them to the people coming off boats. There was such a demand for the juices that I'd come back quickly after selling them, and wash the glasses for another round, while Soronjita was blending more juice.

Following our success, other people started imitating us, also having kids sell juices for them. They'd even go to the port saying it was juice from my bar La Vitamina, and then when I went to the port people had already bought juice thinking that it was mine. Unfortunately, this new competition cut into our business, so we decided to open a restaurant. I worked in the restaurant for three years doing the cooking since I was good at seasoning. I also hired a very good cook from the northern part of Peru, who taught me many new dishes and techniques. Saturday nights were the busiest. Unfortunately this cook would get drunk on Saturdays and he wouldn't show up at work. Taking his cooking secrets, I ended up doing all the cooking, with the result that my restaurant became very famous, and everybody in the town came to eat there often, because there weren't too many other restaurants.

After more than two years of running the restaurant, I got tired of it, and began losing the desire to work. One night I had a dream, in which my grandmother came and showed me seven different roots of the *renaco* tree, which had beautiful and graceful forms. Then she said, "That's what you should do, son. I give it to you as a gift." In the dream, I was grateful to my grandmother for the gift. I put the roots on my shoulder, and every piece gave off a wonderful sound, like bells and kettledrums, that penetrated my being.

Afterwards, I woke up inspired, at 1:00 in the morning, and began to paint. I had paint left over from having painted the tables and benches for the restaurant. The first painting I did was of three people from the Shipibo tribe, an Indian man with his wife and child. I was very involved with the problems of the Shipibos, because I liked this tribe very much.

I also began looking around for a shaman and I met a *maestro ayahuasquero*, whose name was William Guevara. He was a Campa

Indian, who had taken the last name of his patron, because he didn't have one of his own. In those days, the Indians worked with people from England and Spain, collecting animal skins, and extracting wood from the jungle, and they would acquire the surnames of their employers. I began attending ceremonies to drink *ayahuasca* with him, because I wanted to see through the ceremonies the meaning of my dream about those root forms, and I knew that the *ayahuasca* could give me the best guidance.

In an *ayahuasca* ceremony with William Guevara, I had a very powerful vision of a demon who was shooting fire from it's mouth; the flames would stop half a meter away from me and then return to the demon's mouth. It was a friendly and striking demon, with big, fiery eyes colored red, blue, and green. It had colorful horns, and rays coming out of its body. Its image made me laugh loudly while William Guevara was singing and dancing. Annoyed, he admonished me, and asked why I was laughing so hard. I explained to him there was a demon making me laugh. "You're the demon," I told him, "because when you're dancing I can see the demon."

"Ahh," he said, "that's my demon."

When I had arrived at the ceremony, there were some sick people within their mosquito nets, complaining about their pains. After William Guevara called attention to me, I realized all the sick people were laughing hard as well. Being contagious, my laughter had healed them, and William Guevara acknowledged this unexpected turn of events, telling me my laughter had cured these patients.

The ceremony continued with beautiful singing and dancing. His *icaros* (the magical tunes that are used by *ayahuasqueros* in their ceremonies or healings) and *mariris* (magical songs) were very beautiful. William Guevara was a good *brujo*, who could use his powers to heal, but he could be a vengeful and dangerous *brujo* as well.

Then I had a vision of flying in outer space, watching many different kinds of planets passing by. I headed towards a very big planet, then gravity started pulling me even closer to it, and I couldn't get out of its gravitational field. I saw a big tunnel with a light deep inside, and I thought to myself the only thing I could do not to crash into this planet — because I was flying at great speed — was to go into the tunnel. So I entered the tunnel, and in seconds I was in the center of the planet, in a place of pure fire. Because it was burning me, I began to shout.

"What's happening?" William said, coming over.

"I'm inside a planet, and it's burning me!"

Again William Guevara admonished me for making too much noise, which he thought was making the patients tense. But when I told William what had happened, the patients began to laugh again.

Soon it was almost dawn, and the ceremony was over. The ceremony had been one of the best experiences of my life. I considered the significance of what had happened to me in my visions, as William didn't explain the meaning to me. Such teachers do not explain visions, leaving interpretations up to individual participants in the ceremonies.

As far as I was concerned, my spirit had left my body and gone looking for its place of origin, in outer space. After this experience I resolved to continue with more *ayahuasca* ceremonies to make additional discoveries.

William Guevara always came to my restaurant to eat, but I wouldn't charge him because he was a *maestro*, a *brujo*. One day when he was there, he ordered a beer. I was a bit annoyed that day because many people hadn't paid me, and I was feeling irritated. When I told him I couldn't give him a beer, he was angry and told me that as a result my restaurant was going to fail, that I would lose customers.

From that day my business started to decline rapidly, as if he had jinxed it. This was eerie since my restaurant was usually filled with people.

Then it was time for the Pucallpa Fair, where I built my own stand, and exhibited some sculptures I had created with *renaco* roots. On two occasions my grandmother had come to me in dreams, telling me to make these sculptures. In addition I had made a beautiful, huge mahogany table, from one piece of trunk. I also had killed a hundred chickens to cook and sell at the fair, storing them in the refrigerators at my house. On the day of the fair there was no electricity in the town, so the chickens went bad and I had a loss in that business.

When I exhibited the sculptures, some newspaper reporters did a story about my work, although I made no profit from them at the fair.

Shortly thereafter I continued work at the restaurant. One day I invited some friends I had met at the fair, writers, artists, and one film actor, to come to the restaurant, and they were all drunk when they arrived. In addition to being artists, they were socialists who always talked about Che Guevara. I told them that I had one of Che Guevara's berets he had given me and brought it out to show them. There was also a man named Kunti, who had been in the war with Che Guevara. He took the beret from me to look at it, went to the bathroom, and came out without it. I believe he hid the beret in his clothes. In any case, I never saw the beret again and I lost my only remembrance from Che Guevara.

Business at the restaurant continued to decline until there were virtually no customers. So I agreed to rent the restaurant to a friend, Javier. He and his wife, Ruth removed my business name, which was "La Vitamina", and named it "El Che Che Room". After he had worked there about three months, he saw the business wasn't working for him either. Apparently the *brujo* had jinxed the place entirely. As a result, in 1969 I closed the restaurant for good.

I had transported all the materials I had used to construct my booth at the fair to an area of land I had bought on the Yarinacocha highway. There I built a workshop in which to create my sculptures.

One day I was working on the figure of a wooden Shipibo Indian, and some Shipibo Indians came by to see the sculpture. For some reason they didn't like the fact that I was working on a piece concerning them, and like a curse, a type of whirlwind, called a *muruhuayra*, began. It lifted my house completely off the ground, leaving only the sculpture standing. However, with the remaining pieces of the roof I built another house and kept on working.

In those times hordes of hippies from Argentina, Brazil, Chile, and Ecuador, would come to Pucallpa looking for mushrooms and other plants to eat, investigating whatever they could learn about hallucinogenic plants and the related culture. They'd often stay at my workshop on the Yarinacocha highway, sometimes bringing mushrooms with them as well as *isangos* (very tiny insects that can hardly be seen which cause itching), on their bodies. I first experienced mushrooms through contact with these hippies. After eating more than twenty, I fell dizzy to the floor, and everything in the room was physically transformed into a visionary world. People's faces appeared like ovals, with huge mouths and eyes.

Although I tried to feed these poor hippies and help them to survive, it was difficult for me to create my sculptures with so many people coming to my workshop. I finally left and went back to my house in Pucallpa. It was on Jiron Tarapaca Road, where I have a big house today, but back then I had a very small house. There I continued working on my sculptures with more solitude.

Chapter 13

Introduction to the Realm of Ayahuasca

Around this time I decided to see a *brujo* for help in alleviating headaches and acidity I was experiencing, and to improve my creativity.

I was told that on the outskirts of Pucallpa there was a healer called Don Ramon, and I went to visit him. When I told him what my problem was he was very friendly and offered to help, telling me to come the next day for an *ayahuasca* ceremony to cure me. This was the beginning of my formal studies with *ayahuasca*.

The next evening, I arrived with two Argentineans, a wife and husband, and there were other people there as well. Altogether there were about eight of us who participated.

After I drank the *ayahuasca*, I began to have marvelous visions of colored snakes, and then I felt like vomiting. I went outside to vomit, because there were no buckets indoors in which to vomit. I remember I leaned on a tree trunk dropping my pants, shitting at the same time I vomited. I was afraid I'd fall into my own excrement. After vomiting I somehow pulled my pants back on, although I didn't know where my hands were, as I was so disconnected to my body.

Then I went back to the living room because Don Ramon was calling me. "Sit down," he said. During Don Ramon's ceremony, we sat on the bare floor since there were no cushions or benches. The mosquitoes were biting us, but I was having very good visions, seeing serpents, spirits, and other fascinating images.

After everything was over, at about three or four in the morning, Don Ramon said to me, "You have a good spirit, I like very much how you behaved last night. Next Friday we'll have another ceremony, and you should come."

"Okay, Don Ramon," I answered.

He asked me for my home address and came looking for me on the morning of the next ceremony when I was working on my sculptures.

"Good morning! How are the headaches?" he asked me.

"I don't have them anymore," I answered.

"Good. Don't forget that today we'll have another *ayahuasca* ceremony, so come."

Without headaches, I could now work really well. I had many bottles of plant liquors at home that I used to sell when I had the restaurant, and I invited Don Ramon to try some. After tasting it, he didn't want to leave, and when he finished one bottle, he wanted another.

"Don Ramon, aren't we having a ceremony tonight?" I asked.

"Yes, I'd better go," he said, "otherwise I'll get drunk here. I'll be waiting for you because I like your presence in the ceremony. You are a light!"

I was actually more interested in working on my sculptures that night, but, at the same time, I felt that a magnet was pulling me, like a boa luring me with it's magnetism, so I decided to go.

When I arrived at about eight that evening, lots of people were already there. Don Ramon gave me very preferential treatment, thanking me for coming and referring to me affectionately as "Aguchito."

He said, "Aguchito, you're a good element, and you'll learn here. Make yourself comfortable, and put up your mosquito net to rest after the ceremony is over."

Don Ramon left for his room to fetch his instruments. He set up his *mesa* (ceremonial table), and placed the bottle of *ayahuasca* on it. He didn't have any *shacapa* (dried leaves that are bunched together and shaken as a musical instrument), or *maracas* (gourds used as rattles), since he didn't use them in his ceremonies. He only had his *arco* (a bow-shaped musical string instrument), pipe, perfumes, and tobacco.

Don Agustin's boat which carries groups back and forth from Iquitos to Tamshiyacu.

Don Agustin's jungle camp Yushintaita.

Don Agustin playing his drum at his jungle retreat Yushintaita.

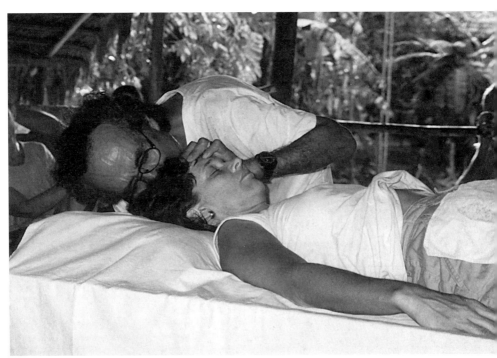

Don Agustin healing a patient.

Don Agustin praying with a flower from the *toé* (datura) plant, before adding it to an *ayahuasca* brew that he was preparing.

The enormous *shiwahuaco* tree within which 20 standing people could fit, at Don Agustin's first encampment near Pucallpa.

Selecting the *ayahuasca* vines to take.

Blowing smoke to thank t
ayahuasca before cutting

Playing an *icaro* and *mariri*
to thank the *ayahuasca*.

Don Agustin and helper preparing the *ayahuasca* to be cooked.

One of Don Agustin's helpers preparing the *ayahuasca* to be cooked.

Ayahuasca cooking.

Don Agustin with his two assistant *ayahuasqueros*, Luis Panduro Vasquez and Artidoro Perdomo Rodriguez, preparing the ceremonial *mesa* for an *ayahuasca* ceremony.

Don Agustin at his ceremonial *mesa*.

Don Agustin playing the *antara*.

Don Agustin pouring *ojé* (the latex from a tree that is used to kill worms and parasites) preparing for people to drink.

The author Jaya Bear with Don Agustin at his jungle encampment Yushintaita.

Some of the sculptures carved by Don Agustin now on display in the gallery at his house in Pucallpa.

When he began the ceremony, I carefully watched how he took the bottle of *ayahuasca*, how he would blow, and how he would *icaro* (whistle his magical songs). Closing his eyes, he blew into the bottle's neck as if he were spitting in it. He also blew into the cup in which he would serve the *ayahuasca*.

He called me to take the first cup, and after I had drunk he blew tobacco smoke into it. It was a big cup, and the *ayahuasca* was strong. By the time the other ten or twelve people were done, I was already intoxicated. He had to blow the cup for each person he'd serve it to, and then fill it up with *ayahuasca*. It took about fifteen minutes for everybody to drink, and by that time the first person who had drunk was already having visions.

I was seeing serpents, demons, angels, and all kinds of colorful images. After Don Ramon determined we were seeing, he said, "Okay, let's turn off the light," and he put out the kerosene lamp. He remained silent and very focused while filling his pipe with tobacco. He seemed to be thinking about something. I could see his finger, as it was a clear night, pressing the tobacco in, and then as he blew a magical intent onto the pipe with his breath. Then taking a *mapacho* (hand-rolled cigarette of jungle tobacco), he blew smoke around the room to protect it from any bad spirits entering into the space. When everyone was well into their visions, he left the house.

He himself didn't drink *ayahuasca*, although he'd drink *camalonga*, a drink made of seeds, or some other drink which didn't induce any visions. When I asked him, "What are you drinking, Don Ramon?" he'd reply, "My medicine." Certainly he had drunk *ayahuasca* before, when he was younger. Today I can well understand why he sometimes refrained from drinking *ayahuasca* himself. At times I too don't want to drink it, because it can be too much *ayahuasca* for my body when I have already drunk it thousands of times. The *maestro* cannot afford to get dizzy and fall down during a ceremony in front of his patients or students. Otherwise he would lose all of his power.

It appeared this was the case with Don Ramon, that he didn't drink the *ayahuasca* when we did because he was being careful not to lose control and fall down. Instead, he would laugh at us when people vomited and fell down. However, I never fell to the floor, and that's one reason Don Ramon liked me so much.

As the night passed I had many visions of flights in outer space, *Yacurunas* (river spirits), *Sirenas* (mermaids), cats, jaguars, dogs, wolves, elephants, giraffes, and various other animals.

At one point Don Ramon told me to remove my shirt. I felt his hands touching me, and then he blew a perfume all over my body. Whenever I did a ceremony with him, he'd always do this to me, but not to anyone else, unless someone had paid to have a healing. Mostly people paid five or ten *soles* just to drink *ayahuasca*, but not for healing. For healing Don Ramon would charge a hundred or two hundred *soles*, and the sick person had to lay within a mosquito net during the ceremony, rather than sit with the other people.

In this ceremony, there were ill people within their mosquito nets, and at times Don Ramon would work with the patients, saying, "Today the spirit will come to cure you. Your ailments are not serious, you'll heal. The water spirits, the *Yacurunas* will come, or the *Silfos*, *Nereidas*, or *Ondinas* (all spirits of the air), or the *Chullachaqui*, will come to heal you." I also heard him sucking the sicknesses out of their bodies.

At times other than during *ayahuasca* ceremonies, women would also come to Don Ramon to ask him to cast a spell to attract the man they wanted, because he knew how to do this.

In all the times I drank *ayahuasca* with Don Ramon, I never learned his *mariris* (magical songs) or his *icaros* (magical tunes). These are the tunes and songs which an *ayahuasquero* or *brujo* sings to summon the power of plant spirits and other spirits. I never dared to ask about them, since I felt that he didn't want anyone learning his *mariris* or his *icaros*.

Despite this, I gained considerable knowledge by being there and continued to participate in more ceremonies. Don Ramon wouldn't do a ceremony without me, coming to my home the day of a ceremony and asking me to be present. It was almost an obligation for me to go, but he would heal me at each ceremony.

Meanwhile, I also continued to sculpt with *renaco* roots. These roots have marvelous, human-like, beautiful forms. I began to experiment more and more with various techniques to work with them most advantageously, such as peeling the wood or knocking off the bark.

My friends Roger and Javier, who were writing for magazines, frequently wrote news about my work, and I had an exhibition of my works at the Pucallpa Chamber of Commerce. Although the exhibition was a significant event for me, it got mixed reactions, with not everyone admiring my sculptures.

Roger, who lived in Lima, arranged an exhibition for me, set up in the house of another sculptor, Victor Delfin, in Barranco. So in 1971, I prepared to make my first trip to Lima to show my sculptures.

When I told Don Ramon about the exhibition, he said, "If you want to sell your artwork, bring me some perfume." After looking in the stores for a perfume called Bride's Flower Bouquet, I took it to him, but he said, "You only brought one? I also need one for myself."

I answered, "Don Ramon, I'm sorry. I'll go immediately to Pucallpa and get another perfume." As I rode the six kilometers on my bicycle, I realized Don Ramon wanted something more from me, that he also needed money, perfumes, tobacco, shoes, and pants. From that time on, whenever he prepared my perfume, I brought him some gifts.

After I returned with the perfume, he prepared it by blowing his *icaros* into it. I then used the perfume to anoint each of my sculptures that I was exhibiting, with a drop on my finger. He'd say, "This is for you to sell your art work." I believed him with all my heart.

Soon I left for Lima to exhibit in the first Amazonian Art Festival, which my friend Roger had helped to organize, and which was sponsored by the Bubinsana group from Iquitos.

Fortunately for artists at that time, during the presidencies of Fernando Belaunde Terri and Alan Garcia, the government had given the order for the armed forces and the police to be helpful to artists by giving them support, such as flying them to exhibitions in Lima and Iquitos. So, if I needed transportation from Pucallpa to Lima I'd only have to ask, and they'd take me there for free.

Before I left for Lima, when I went to say good-bye to Don Ramon, he said, "When you're a success, remember the poor people, Aguchito." He somehow knew that I was going to excel.

The exhibition took place at the home of Victor Delfin, who sculpted with iron. His house was beautiful, and he'd created an exciting ambiance, putting his sculptures near the quay with colored lights by the ocean. There was entertainment and some of the guests were cultural attachés. All the ambassadors and consulates had been invited to the exhibition, as well as many important people from the Peruvian literary and artistic world.

The exhibition lasted for sixteen days, and during that time I sold almost all my sculptures, although the painters, Ildebrando Rios Valderama and Eduardo Mesa, sold nothing. I was the first artist in Peru to create sculptures out of *renaco* roots, and for this reason I became the best known sculptor from the Amazon.

My wife and I were invited to dinner by the German ambassador, and later the German government invited me to exhibit my work in Germany.

From that moment on, I held Don Ramon in great esteem, because I believed he had made it possible for me to sell my sculptures. I also realized more and more how much my work with Don Ramon had affected my sculpting. I increasingly respected him as a *maestro* and continued visiting him at his encampment near the Pucallpa airport where he'd teach me about the uses of various plants.

Every time we drank *ayahuasca* at his camp, we'd wait for the arrival and departure of the planes. They'd arrive at about nine at night, and then they'd take off for Lima. Then we'd take advantage of the silence and start the ceremony.

Much later when he had health problems the tables were turned, and Don Ramon asked my help in finding a cure. His health problems began when his son assaulted him with a branch from a *piñon colorado* plant because he had heard from other people that Don Ramon was having sexual relations with his daughters. The daughters were always close to their father, and Don Ramon was unaware of what people were saying until the day his son assaulted him. Later Don Ramon claimed this was not true. He told me crying, "It's a big lie, what they are saying about me. I would never have sex with my daughters. Sometimes my daughters come to my bed in the way that daughters would come to their father, but never have I had sex with them." From the day of the assault on, he developed a permanent illness, turning yellow and losing his appetite. When a person is attacked with *piñon colorado*, the individual generally becomes ill and eventually dies.

Don Ramon told me he had gone to friends who knew how to cure this problem, but that none of the medicines of the *brujos* had produced results.

Then he told his wife, "Perhaps if I go to Don Agustin he can cure me." She agreed, so he came to my house. He was very yellow and swollen. I told him the alcohol he drank was also hurting him. When I started to blow tobacco smoke on him as a method of healing, he fainted and fell to the floor. I continued blowing smoke on him, doing the work to heal his body. After a while he regained some strength and returned to his camp. Because he was a master of medicine, I had great respect for him and offered to come do a healing later that night.

I realized I had to have some powerful magic for Don Ramon to recover confidence in his life. I had studied different magical techniques from books, and I decided to create a circle and a cross within the circle.

When I arrived at his camp, Don Ramon was in bed, but felt better because the treatment was already working. I said to him, "I have come to cure you."

"The doctors have told me this cannot be cured," he responded. I disagreed, insisting that his illness could be cured, but told him he'd have to have faith in me.

He remarked, "Since I went to your house I do feel better. What are you going to do to me? Help your teacher?"

"Don Ramon, the teacher sometimes needs help from the

student," I affirmed.

"If I would have gone to you earlier, I wouldn't have gotten this sick. But I went to other *brujos* like me who don't know anything," said Don Ramon.

So we both drank a cup of *ayahuasca* and entered into a different state of consciousness. I made a circle with a cross in the center then asked him if the son who had assaulted him had some clothing or shoes in the house.

"Yes, his clothes are here. He left after hitting me with the branch of *piñon colorado*," Don Ramon said.

"Your son needs to come on his knees, to beg your forgiveness," I told him.

Then I put his son's clothes and old shoes in the center of the cross and set them on fire. We waited until they had burned to ashes.

"All right, Don Ramon, go around the circle," I instructed him. He began to walk first around the circle from left to right, then from right to left. Next I told him to jump over the fire in various directions. Then I asked him to walk around the circle again. Finally, I told him to step onto the fire, which he did. "You have to put it out, Don Ramon," I said, singing *mariris*. Don Ramon began to sweat profusely. Once he had put out the fire, we threw away the ashes, and Don Ramon went to bed. I told him the next day he'd feel better.

The next day, at sunrise, I told him, "All right, today you are going to begin to heal." I remained there until midday watching how he was responding. Then Don Ramon sat up in his bed, smiled and said, "Agustin. I feel better!"

By now Don Ramon looked less yellow than before. Satisfied that I had helped, I then told him I had to go to work on some sculptures to sell.

At home, while resting before sculpting, I began to dream about Don Ramon. In the dream a spirit told me the treatment I had given him would be helpful. I awoke about eight that evening and then began to do some work on a sculpture.

At about nine the next morning, Don Ramon arrived. He was

very tranquil and told me he felt good, with no symptoms of vomiting or headaches.

I took out a bottle of medicine containing several plants, which, when put into a cane liquor, results in a extract beneficial to health and virility. My mother and my grandfather always used it as a medicine to give one strength. The mixture contained *ipururu*, a plant that grows on lake banks, *achunisanango*, a plant which grows along the edges of small creeks and has the properties of being a stimulant for the body in general, principally the nervous system, and *tamamuri*, a large forest tree with buttressed roots used on its own for rheumatism. Don Ramon and I drank the medicine until we finished the bottle and were a bit tipsy. Don Ramon began to laugh, enjoying the new health he had acquired after the treatment.

The next day, when I went to the market, I met his son and asked, "Have you asked forgiveness from your father for what you have done?"

"No, Don Agustin. It weighs heavy on me, and I am ashamed for what I've done. I want to go to my father, but I'm afraid."

"Come with me," I said. "You should kneel down and ask your father's forgiveness for assaulting him with the *piñon colorado*. I know the whole story, and your father has never had sex with his daughters."

Then we went to Don Ramon's house. When he saw his son, he was annoyed, but I told him I had brought his son to ask his forgiveness.

"All right then, kneel there!" said Don Ramon. The young man kneeled before his father. "Now I'm going to give you five beltings for what you have done to me. That is the only way I'll forgive you." This he did, and afterwards the young man hugged his father, and they forgave each other. I left for my house, and they remained there together.

Days passed, and I kept working on my sculptures, creating some for an exhibition in Lima. A few days later I went to Don Ramon's and found them happy. He had taken his son to the university and enrolled him again. He had been at the university before his assault on his father but then dropped out and wandered in the streets like a crazy person. Now he was also helping his father prepare for *ayahuasca* ceremonies, splitting the wood, lighting the fire, and chopping the *ayahuasca*. Don Ramon was very happy he had been able to re-establish a relationship with his son and that his son was serving him, as well as studying. And I was happy that I had been able to help Don Ramon regain his health. At ninety, he is still alert and strong.

Chapter 14
The Enormous Shiwahuaco Tree

One day I was working in my studio in Yarinacocha near Pucallpa, on the edge of the lake where I had bought ten hectares of land, when a young man from Canada arrived. His name was Benjamin, and his father was an ambassador in another South American country. Although Benjamin was nineteen years old and seemed healthy, he had come requesting a healing. I told him I didn't have time to cure him because I was busy making sculptures, so he left.

A year later he reappeared while I was again working in my studio, and said, "Don Agustin, this time I want you to heal me."

"All right," I agreed, "I'll work a little more and then we'll return to Pucallpa." It was about six kilometers from the lake to Pucallpa. After I finished working, we bathed in the lake, and I observed that Benjamin was spinning around like a top. It turned out he was suffering from an illness that would make him spin around and fall down in the middle of the street. Although he'd been to various hospitals, none of the doctors had been able to cure him. His father had given him money to go to other healers in Africa, Brazil, Ecuador, and India to look for a cure, but so far no one had been able to heal him.

That night he slept in a hammock at my house, and because he had placed it too high he fell from it like a cat, standing. He was agile.

The next day I asked him to go look for *ayahuasca* since I didn't have any.

"Where am I going to find it?" he questioned.

"Asking and asking you can arrive in Rome. That is, by asking and asking, you'll find where there is *ayahuasca*," I replied.

"All right," he said. He left my house in Pucallpa at eight in the morning, and by four that afternoon he returned, dirty and perspiring, with a bottle of *ayahuasca*.

"Where did you find it?" I asked.

"Ah, asking and asking I arrived in Rome," he replied.

"Okay, tomorrow we'll go to the jungle where I have a camp with a huge *shiwahuaco* tree," I told him.

"There's a friend who wants to go with me. His name is Lucio, and he's an Argentinean," Benjamin answered.

I agreed, and the next morning the three of us took the omnibus from Pucallpa, enjoying the views we passed. After riding sixty-seven kilometers, we got off and walked to the Moronillo River. The river was high, and we had to swim across since we didn't have a boat. Our bags had been put in plastic bags so we used them to help us swim to the other side, where we put on dry clothes.

After walking another ten kilometers and passing the house of my Aunt Rogelia, who gave us some chicken to eat, we finally arrived at the camp. At that time it was still all jungle. The encampment which I built later, didn't exist yet. There was only a huge *shiwahuaco* tree which was big enough that twenty standing people could fit inside of it.

"Where are we going to sleep?" they asked.

"Here, inside the tree. Let's clean it," I answered. It was already two in the afternoon, so we quickly started to clean it, using leafy branches to sweep out the tree which was covered with bat excrement.

I'd previously made a door in the tree, of branches tied together with wire, to prevent jaguars from entering, and there were two cots with mosquito nets inside. I slept in one, and Benjamin and his friend Lucio slept on the other. In the darkness we could hear bats flying around. We had put plastic over the mosquito nets to keep the bat excrement from falling onto us, and we could hear the bats hiding fruits in the plastic wrap. The next morning, after breakfast, we cleaned up the area, sweeping away all the underbrush to keep away spiders and snakes.

For lunch we cooked rice, vermicelli, and *yuca*s, eating it with crackers and milk. We rested most of the afternoon, then bathed in the river. When the sun set, we placed our ceremonial table in front of the water.

That night was very dark, and we drank the *ayahuasca*, which was very strong. In my vision, I saw the trees moving toward us. I spoke to them, telling them not to squeeze us, that we didn't want to harm them, but were there to heal a person. When I looked over Benjamin's head, I saw seven gigantic black gorillas with pointed heads and large shining eyes like lights. I asked them not to harm us, and they remained all night just watching what we were doing. Benjamin and Lucio also saw them.

A little later, when I got up, my legs were shaking. I was feeling very drunk from the visions. I looked into Benjamin's head, and saw his brain like a light, very clearly. Sitting in his brain was a little green leaf. The borders of the leaf were serrated and looked like they had been cut. I told Benjamin that I'd found his illness, and he asked me to pull it out of him. I then drank a little more *ayahuasca* to induce a little vomit or excretion of a magical phlegm called *yachai*. I belched this magical phlegm onto Benjamin's head, then sucked it back into my mouth. Something came out of his head. It didn't feel like a leaf but, rather, like something similar to a clock battery. It was round, cold, and made a metallic noise between my teeth. With my tongue I could feel it in my mouth, and I swallowed it, knowing that if it was good it would stay, but if it was bad it would be expelled. One must be a shaman to do this. If the object is beneficial, it stays inside giving the shaman more energy when the illness is cured. About ten minutes later, my stomach started to move and make sounds; I vomited, feeling the object come out and clink against my teeth. Shining my flashlight, I started poking through the vomit with a little stick, but I couldn't find anything, so I covered it with a towel and decided I'd look again in the morning. We continued with the ceremony for one or two more hours. I sang until our intoxication had passed, and then we went to bed. In my sleep I dreamed about the object that had been in Benjamin's brain.

When I woke up early the next morning, I went over to Benjamin's bed to see how he was doing, but only Lucio was there. Benjamin was by the river, getting in and out of the water, but his body wasn't spinning around as usual. I observed him for a while, hiding behind a tree for about half an hour, to make sure that he didn't have a twirling fit.

He walked by me, apparently without seeing me, so I went over to him to say hello. He remembered me but said he didn't know where he was and couldn't remember how he had gotten there. He acknowledged he had been ill, but said he now felt more centered.

In the meantime, Lucio had gotten up and gone to look for the object in the vomit. He said that he could feel the object under the towel, but when he took the towel off, there wasn't anything there.

At that time Benjamin didn't pay me for the ceremony, but just told me he really liked the tree. Then he and Lucio returned to Lima, and Benjamin left for Canada. A month later he sent me a money order for $250 from Canada with a note saying, "Many thanks for healing me. I have been working planting trees, and this is the money I made. Please don't let anyone destroy that tree."

With the money he gave me, I built a house and established a healing encampment in the jungle by this tree. It was good land and I also planted *ayahuasca*, pineapples, fruit, rice, and corn.

Chapter 15
Shamanic Training Through Plant Diets

One beautiful, warm day in 1975, I was on the way to my healing encampment. It was during a five-year period of rigorous dieting with plants, which I was undergoing as part of my training to become a healer. Over these five years I lived in complete solitude during the periods when I was in my encampment, broken up by an occasional return to my family, to replenish my stock of basic foods and to work at my sculptures for a few weeks. My wife would sell the sculptures in my absence to make money for the family's daily needs.

At midday, feeling tired after having walked for more than an hour, I sat down by a tree to rest and smoke my pipe. The *chicharras* (cicadas), were chirping shrilly up in the trees, and I was enjoying the sounds of the jungle around me, when suddenly, a small man came out of a large tree about thirty meters away. He appeared young, yet had the face of an old man. He had a fine, curved nose, a very small mouth, and was missing one foot. Although he was dressed normally in a shirt, old pants, and an old cloth hat, I knew right away that he was the *Chullachaqui* who I'd spent many years trying to encounter. Not letting him out of my sight and running so that I wouldn't lose him, I said, "Finally I've found you!"

"You have no fear?" he asked me.

"No, I'm not afraid. I've always wanted to meet you, and finally I have. You are the *Chullachaqui* and my friend."

"Yes, and you are Agustin Rivas." The jungle spirit knew my name.

I said, "My friend, I love you."

"I know," he said, shrugging his shoulders. He smiled with his small mouth and long nose, and fixed his gaze on me. His eyes were small and brilliant. I was so happy to have met with the *Chullachaqui* that I never considered the possibility he would steal me away, although that was possible. The *Chullachaqui* can appear to anyone in the guise of a person very familiar to that individual, or as a fierce beast, and then lead the person away or kill them.

My pipe had plenty of tobacco, and standing only about a meter away from him, I asked, "Do you want to smoke my pipe?"

"Yes, good," he said. Then, lifting a shoulder and smiling almost timidly, he took my pipe from me and smoked it.

I said to myself, "How wonderful, he is smoking my pipe!" I was filled with happiness.

He put his hand into a little bag that was hanging from his shoulder and took out a small pipe made out of the seed from a *huicungo*, a palm tree with seeds half the size of a hen's egg. He filled the pipe with *sorrapa*, a hot, and bitter-tasting but delicious green moss that grows on the trees during the rainy season. Then he took the pipe with one hand, and with the other hand, gave it a quick blow, lighting it magically without any flame.

"How did you light your pipe?" I asked.

"That is my own trick. Don't ask too much. I would like you to also smoke my pipe," he answered.

"Oh yes, it is an honor for me to smoke your pipe." I eagerly inhaled the smoke, which tasted of wood and leaves.

Then he taught me about what kind of *sorrapa* he smoked and others that existed, saying, "There are seven kinds of *sorrapas*. One is from a palm tree, another is from very thick trees, and still others are from thin trees, as well as from trees that grow by riverbanks."

Meanwhile, I was enjoying smoking the pipe, and noting how simple it was. The seed had a hole for the tobacco, and another small hole for the mouthpiece, which was made out of some small animal's leg bone. Then I told the *Chullachaqui* I was having no luck hunting lately, that whenever I'd shoot at an animal, I would never hit it. He replied, "Those are my animals. You need to ask my permission first, and you have never asked me before shooting an animal. But today you're going to kill an animal."

Soon I felt the earth was spinning, with the trees turning around me. His face was changing, and he was laughing out loud. After a while I started losing control, my knees were unstable, and I fell to the ground.

Later, when I opened my eyes, the *Chullachaqui* wasn't there, and I got a little scared. I wondered if I had been asleep, then I remembered I'd become unconscious. I had been there about two hours according to the sun's position. I stood up, stumbling a bit, and called out, "*Chullachaqui*! Come back, let's talk some more." But he didn't reappear.

So I picked up my rifle and headed for my encampment. After I had walked for about twenty meters, a very large deer appeared very close to me, looking at me sideways. I aimed my rifle, and shot. After leaping, the deer fell in front of me. I remembered what the *Chullachaqui* had told me about the changing of my hunting luck and said, "Thank you *Chullachaqui*, you gave me what I wanted. I hope I see you again, but the next time you come as a human, not as an animal." No one answered. I tied up the deer's front legs with the back legs, and carried him, almost running, along the path.

By the time I arrived at my encampment an hour and a half later, it was very late. The sun was about to set, and the sky was a beautiful blue with the first evening star already appearing. After sharpening my knife, I started to skin the deer as quickly as I could. I lit my kerosene lamp, and with it's light, finished quartering the animal. I didn't wash the meat, to prevent it from rotting, but only dried off the blood with an old pair of pants, then hung it. I noticed that the bullet had hit the heart precisely, proof to me that the deer had been sent by the *Chullachaqui* as a gift to me.

After a while I was hungry and removed the liver and heart, pierced them with a stick, salted them lightly, and roasted them over the fire together with plantains. After eating I made myself a drink from a plant, called *isulasacha*, which I drank every night. It is a very tasty plant similar to an orange. Then I hummed and sang my *icaros* and *mariris*, which I recorded with a small Sony tape recorder, repeatedly listening to them — my method of learning them in those days.

My routine during the five years I was on plant diets was to walk in the jungle during the days, taking my rifle as protection. I usually saw a jaguar's footprints or heard one running close by, but I wasn't afraid because I had the weapon. In the afternoons, I'd roast plantains or cook some rice, without using salt or spices, which was part of the rigorous discipline of my diets. At night I'd sleep in the huge *shiwahuaco* tree and play the *icaros* and *mariris* on my tape recorder.

When I first started living in the jungle, as a protection against the jaguars, I'd made a barrier at the entrance to the tree with some sticks, tied up with wires in a coconut shape. At night I could hear the jaguars walking around the tree in circles, smelling me. Shouting, I'd scare them off and they'd run away. In the tree I felt protected, so I wasn't afraid of the animals.

I was, however, scared of the nights because of other sounds I'd hear. At night all sounds seemed to be louder and echoed in the jungle. Mysteriously, one night when I was recording, I heard a sound like the crack of a whip against a tree. Very frequently I'd hear someone calling my name, "Agustin! Agustin!" I never knew what caused such sounds.

One day I heard an eerie sound like a cow bellowing on the other side of the river, lost in the jungle. It was a rainy and gloomy day, and the river which was about thirty meters away from my encampment, had risen. When I stood up to go and see what was causing the noise my body trembled and I had a distinct feeling that I'd better not go, so I didn't. That night I had strange dreams and had contacts with phantoms, probably because I was there alone drinking *ayahuasca* and the other plants.

During the diet with each plant, in addition to the plant itself, I restricted myself to eating only rice, plantains, mushrooms from the jungle called *callampas*, and non-scavenger fish called *boquichicos*, which don't have teeth or scales and only eat water plants. I refrained entirely from consuming fruits, vegetables, salt or spices. Each diet would last for eight to ninety days depending on the personal commitment I made.

After such plant diets one can enter into an even more intense discipline of dieting in isolation for six months to one year, without meat, salt or sugar — this is to obtain the ultimate level of *banco*. In the Amazon, *banco* is considered the highest level that a shaman or *brujo* can attain. In this state of consciousness the *brujo* has acquired many spiritual powers, powers of healing, and the ability to assume the body of any bird, animal or fish, using it as a vehicle to travel by land, air or water.

The *maestros*, Don Ramon and William Guevara had taught me the process of how to diet with many of the different plants. They both felt I had a good spirit and great potential for becoming a healer. I felt privileged because, out of many people who were participating in the *ayahuasca* ceremonies, Don Ramon gave me preferential treatment. For example, calling me to the center of the room, he'd cover my body with an aromatic substance he'd prepared to ward off dangers, to protect me, and to bring me health. I realized he would give me the help I needed to have endurance if I decided to pursue the work of a shaman. In addition to dieting with plants to become a healer, another motivation was the enhancement of my creativity. I was deeply immersed in my sculpting, and during these diets I carved many sculptures. I still have one of them I made during that time, at my home in Pucallpa. It's small but very heavy, made from a *shiwahuaco* root, from the same tree in which I was living. When there was no rain and it was dry, it's roots would go down to the river. Then when the torrential rains came, the river would rise and the very strong currents would uproot the roots, then expose them. That is how I got one of its roots to carve. Each diet enhanced my creative ability to sculpt in a different way, and I was intrigued with the possibilities.

I usually drank each plant I was working with only once at the beginning of the diet. There is no set requirement for how many times you can ingest a plant during the period set aside for such a diet. I could have drunk any plant that I was dieting with every day if I had wanted, but it would no doubt have taken a heavy toll on my body. Drinking a plant only once during that period was often sufficient, because some plants work like vaccinations — their energy and benefits remained with me permanently. During the period of time I had put aside, I maintained an ongoing connection and dialogue with the plant I was working with, and that plant spirit appeared in visions and dreams to teach and give counsel. I would also make a song for each plant that I drank as its magic was passed on to me. The *icaros* would come first, they are the magical tunes without words. Then I would add the *mariris*, the words.

In the periods between each diet meat was permitted, but again, without salt or seasonings, and very well roasted and crunchy, or smoked. I didn't eat it very often, and when I did, it was either deer, monkey or *paucar* (a bird), the jungle animals that are herbivorous. Meat from animals such as pigs or chickens, which are raised in the city, or fish which are scavengers, from the Amazon or the Ucayali, are not eaten. I realized I had to eat some meat between diets, because I knew that I needed to gain my strength back.

The process of dieting with plants to become a healer takes five years because it is only possible to focus on one plant at a time. I began with *ojé*, (the latex from the *ojé* tree), with which I cleansed my body before starting with the other plants. After drinking the *ojé* and going through the intense intestinal cleansing the plant causes, I remained in my bed for eight days, working only with positive thoughts. During this time it is necessary to remain focused on positive thoughts even if one has fear of something like a jaguar on the physical plane, or demons or spirits, like the *Chullachaqui*, the guardian spirit of the jungle, which may also appear.

The next plant I drank was *catahua*, a tree with spines that is very caustic and can burn the intestines like *ojé*. This diet lasted for one month. I took about two spoonfuls of *catahua* resin, and put it in a small cup. Then I placed the cup into a pot of boiling water to heat it. This method of using a double saucepan to heat something is called *baño de maria*. When the *catahua* became slightly thickened like gelatin, I drank it. When it is prepared this way, it doesn't burn the stomach as much as when it's fresh from the tree.

This plant is very strong and protects us from enemies. It helps us become invulnerable, also protecting our body from any *virote* thrown at us by another *brujo*. *Virote* is an imaginary thing or evil thought projected forcefully out through the mouth by a sorcerer, which can hit another person like a dart. Sending such things is also done by many *ayahuasqueros* during an *ayahuasca* ceremony, but only as a means of protection, without malevolent thoughts.

Catahua also strengthens the stomach and the intestine and gives a person a stronger character. After using it, one becomes more of a *brujo*, able to enter into the study of *ayahuasca*. When other shamanic healers or *brujos* know that a person has drunk *catahua*, they have a lot of respect for that individual.

"You've drunk *catahua* and you're not dead? It's very dangerous to drink *catahua*," they will say.

During the month I dieted with *catahua*, I didn't receive any messages from the spirits, or have any visions. The time passed tranquilly with the *catahua* in my body, but afterwards it was like I had an antidote to any spells against me. I felt that if any *brujo* aimed a *virote*, a mental, malevolent dart, at me, it would not reach me, but would deviate from its mark. *Catahua* is always protecting me, and no malicious intent from others can affect me.

There are many other plants that can also protect one, such as tobacco, *ayahuasca*, or *chiriqsanango*. But *catahua* acts specifically as a protection against wounds *brujos* attempt to inflict. In addition, it also teaches an individual how to do harm. However, when I drank *catahua* I didn't have any intention of using it to do evil and I vowed not to. Instead, I drank it to protect my body from any hostile energy invading me.

During this period, I had different types of dreams or visions various nights, depending on what diet I was on. Frequently I dreamed about a very beautiful woman who usually appeared while I was lying in my bed in the mornings, in that state of being almost awake. Lifting the mosquito net, she lay down at my side. I would embrace her to have sex but then wake up, only to see that my arms were in the position of embracing someone. I didn't feel too much disappointment, thinking that she must have appeared for a purpose. When this beautiful woman visited me, I didn't have an erection because Don Ramon had taught me how to prevent erections when I was thinking about my wife, by drinking camphor. Later, I made a wooden sculpture of the beautiful woman in these dreams, a spirit whose name was Yara.

During this time I was alone in the jungle, and my family didn't know if I was alive or dead. My wife Soronjita wanted me to come back home, but she also accepted what I was doing. My family knew how to support themselves while I was in the jungle, and I had left them some sculptures they could sell in order to eat. Every three months I'd return to my family, take them a deer, and get rice and plantains to bring back with me because I didn't have plantains in my encampment.

From the river, I'd hear noises like blows that were maybe caused by boas, alligators, or fishes hitting their tails on the water. It was a narrow river, and in the dry season during the month of June, it would dry up leaving only little holes filled with water. Then I was afraid to drink that water, so on a rainy day I'd collect water in a big piece of plastic, which I'd hollow out and place over a big can. I used that water to drink and to make my *isulasacha* tea.

I could hear jaguars roaring, and sometimes the sound of big trees falling echoed through the jungle. In this way, day after day would pass, and I was very happy living there in the large tree continuing on with my discipline.

My third diet was with *lupuna colorado*, a beautiful, cylindrical tree. I began this diet after a fifteen-day rest, during which I ate meat and other foods, including salt.

Entering into the *lupuna* diet, I first asked permission from the tree to remove its bark, because I felt a lot pain about doing this. Many people do this with a machete without consideration, and they hurt the tree. Instead, I scraped off only the outermost layer of the bark with my machete, gathering it in a plantain leaf and then boiling it. This is the red *lupuna*, also sometimes called the *lupuna bruja*, because when you hit the tree it has a metallic sound as if it were hollow inside, and this sometimes causes rain. The tree is gorgeous, rounded in its lower section and more cylindrical higher up. The *maestros* taught me how to drink the *lupuna*, scraping and grinding it after removing the bark, and then cooking it very well almost like *ayahuasca*.

This diet lasted for a month, and on a special night, I drank the *lupuna*. I had always thought I could die by drinking it, because many people had told me that, but I didn't experience any such danger. In any case, I had made a decision to die or become a good shaman — the attitude that a shamanic student should have. Such an attitude dispels any fear of drinking these plants. In my case it was harder because I was on my own without anybody's help.

After I drank the *lupuna*, I felt as if I had a fever, and my ears were ringing. The nights with *lupuna* were very lucid. I could hear clearly the beautiful songs that came through, and *lupuna* taught me a lot.

I saw the spirit of *lupuna*, who is the same *Chullachaqui* transformed into an old woman. This little old woman had big ears, a long nose, very large eyes, a wrinkled face, and was slightly bent over when she walked but didn't use a walking stick. She brought me a piece of wood in her hands, saying, "This wood is good for you to drink." She taught me about *cahuapuri*, showed me the tree, and said, "Look at this tree, it is *cahuapuri*. You should also drink this after *lupuna*." I obeyed the old lady because she was a messenger of the spirit.

After fifteen days of dieting with *lupuna* I felt that my mind was very potent, with tremendous intuition. From it I also learned about mechanical things, like *trapiches* to grind sugarcane, traps, and other objects which I later made and sold in the market.

When I was finished my diet with *lupuna*, immediately the next day, I started drinking *cahuapuri*, with no rest between diets since the old woman had told me to do this diet immediately, for one month.

I knew the tree, and where to find it. It is a little tree, almost like a *liana*, that always grows by riverbanks. Drinking it can give one mastery over the mind, and the power to heal. After removing the *cahuapuri* bark I didn't boil it, because the old woman had told me not to. Instead, I followed her directions as to its preparation. She had told me to grind it and soak it in water all night, then drink the liquid the next morning.

At that time I weighed fifty kilos and was very thin, but strong. Due to the plant medicines, I had a tremendous imagination and an intense desire to heal people. I greatly respected the plants, and I drank them with gratitude and pleasure.

When I finished with the *cahuapuri* diet, I ate chili, a little salt, lemon, and sugar. Chili is necessary to warm up the body and enter another state to prepare for the next diet.

The shaman has to pace himself, graduating to each new level of knowledge — knowledge given by the spirits. I began at the level of *muraillo*, then after one year I graduated to *muraya*, then to *alto muraya*, and after that to *altomando muraya*. The next level after that is *banco*, the highest level of knowledge. I cannot become a *banco* because I have fear of doing the necessary one year diet at this time. My life involves so much work at the moment, it would be very difficult for me. I would have to separate myself from all people, and be completely isolated for a whole year, talking only with the spirits.

After drinking *cahuapuri*, I was walking in the jungle the next day and I found *ninacaspi*. Four days later I drank it. *Ninacaspi* is like a small bamboo plant. When it is cut with a machete, sparks fly out from it, but they can only be seen when it is dark. The plant has little spores on its long narrow leaves. This is the secret of the plant. *Nina* means fire, and *caspi* means plant or wood. To prepare the drink, I took about twenty thin little sticks with all their leaves and carried them to my encampment, where I pounded them and boiled them. *Ninacaspi* needs to be well-boiled. It has a neutral taste, almost like water.

At what hour should I drink it? I didn't know, because my *maestros* hadn't told me. I had to have my own intuition to learn. Other than some directions on how to prepare a few of the plants, I learned none of the plant knowledge from Don Ramon or the other *maestros*. I learned everything by myself in the jungle, through dieting and drinking the different plants — directly from the spirit of the plants.

I said, "Plant of fire, I'm going to drink you in the morning at sunrise." The next morning I drank it at sunrise. Not knowing what quantity to take, I tried a little taste of it first and decided to drink the whole cup.

Then the effect started to occur, and it felt like there were arrows or worms in my bowels and in my stomach. It felt as though my body was burning up, and flames of fire were coming out of it. I went down to the river and, pounding the water with a stick to make sure there were no eels or alligators, I jumped in and spent about two hours in the water. Afterwards my body was still burning like fire, and I could actually see sparks of fire coming out of it. I also saw a vision of a huge garden of the *ninacaspi* plant, being cultivated by old women who appeared very poor, with hair tied up and big teeth. I was seeing all of this in clear daylight. It wasn't a hallucination, nor was it coming from my imagination, these were visions. I tried to go into the garden, but always, in front of me, blocking my entrance, were *zapote* trees, *guayaba* trees, and pineapple plants. Though the garden kept on receding as I approached, I kept on pursuing it before suddenly finding myself deep in the dense jungle with the owls hooting at me and with no machete or weapon. I knew how to return, although I'd gone very far, more than one kilometer away from my encampment.

After I finished with this diet, I felt that the *ninacaspi* had taught me a lot.

Around this time I often wandered in the jungle, looking at the trees and plants, and sometimes I found *ayahuasca*. Once I found an *ayahuasca* vine by the river. Perhaps a tribe had abandoned it there, because it's difficult for *ayahuasca* to grow where there aren't any people. This *ayahuasca* was very thick and had two or three big *lianas*, or woody vines, like serpents that wound their way up to the tops of trees, almost thirty meters. I started to harvest it from the top; if there are several *lianas*, you start to pick the thinnest ones. You always need to leave the father or mother, the primary and thickest rope.

It was during the beginning of the *ninacaspi* diet when I found the *ayahuasca*, and I thought perhaps the spirits wanted me to drink this particular *ayahuasca*. I had brought a load of *ayahuasca* vines from Pucallpa, and I had them buried in fresh leaves to prevent them from drying out. I also had *ayahuasca* in bottles already prepared, but I wanted to try this *ayahuasca*. It had very pretty pink flowers, which were odorless, helix-shaped, and similar to the flowers brides put on their heads.

That day it was very late and I removed the *lianas* from the *ayahuasca*; they were about an inch in diameter and very mature. This *ayahuasca* must be strong, I thought. I brought the *ayahuasca* back to my encampment. The next day I pounded it until it was well ground, then cooked it in a large pot with about fifty *chacruna* leaves for two days, and it was like honey. Although I didn't add much *chacruna*, I had very good visions when I drank it three days later. Once or twice I drank *ayahuasca* without adding *chacruna* and it didn't have the same effect. The *chacruna* brings the visions, it contains the DMT triptamine, and that's why *ayahuasca* needs *chacruna* to bring us visions.

I heard the *chicua* bird singing it's song, and I knew it was going to be good *ayahuasca*. That evening I prepared myself to drink it, eager to see what visions I would have. Since I was alone, I calculated the right amount to drink so I'd stay in control. I turned on the tape recorder and listened to my *mariris* and drank the *ayahuasca*.

After about half an hour, I started to feel as if both my ears were exploding. It shook my whole body. I could hear the trees falling and the earth roaring, and feel the earth moving. I closed my eyes and started singing a *mariri* that *maestro* Don Adriano Tello used to sing, an old Indian man with whom I had also drunk *ayahuasca*. Singing his music, I began to see him and he said, "Very good, Don Agustin, you're doing really well. Try to keep your body upright. Even if the *ayahuasca* is very strong, don't lie down on your bed or on the floor. Sit and let your head lean forward, never backwards."

"Okay, Don Adriano," I answered. Then Don Adriano was transformed into an elf surrounded by lights. He had swords and rays coming out of his body. I told him, "Thank you for being here." I realized I was talking to my visions, but this prevented me from becoming unconscious.

Next, lightning started flashing in the sky, and different colored lights came at me with great speed from all directions, entering my body. I saw beautiful rainbows with rays of many different colors, more colors than the rainbows we know.

Then I went into the Amazon River, seeing mermaids and men with fish tails and red eyes looking at me. They spoke to me, saying, "You are Agustin Rivas, and you are going to be a great master. We are going to introduce you to our empire." They grabbed my hand and took me beneath the waters. Oh, how beautiful it was to see within the Amazon River! There were buildings and beautiful women dancing in front of me, wearing celestial dresses of clear pink, and dresses made of algae with diamonds, snails and precious stones. They were riding on the backs of large serpents and invited me to journey with them. Sitting on these women's tails, I was traveling within the water of my vision. We entered into a very dark tunnel, so obscure we couldn't see anything, and then with great speed we came out into another place within the water. They showed me some stainless steel objects, which looked like spaceships. I got into one of them and we launched into outer space, traveling with great speed, seeing stars and planets. In the spaceship, I listened to the *Yacurunas* who were traveling with me, singing the most beautiful and marvelous songs, and I took many excerpts from them to use in my own *mariris*.

When I woke up from these visions, it was about three or four in the morning, and I realized I'd had no concept of how the time had passed during that *ayahuasca* ceremony. It was as if I had just gone to bed, slept and awakened, except that I had had visions. I then went to sleep, and had no more visions or dreams, and awoke at about nine in the morning feeling good.

Since the *ayahuasca* had been so wonderful, I put what was left over in a bottle to keep. It wouldn't go bad because the jungle was cool, and the *ayahuasca* stayed under the leaves in the shade of the tree where I lived.

After dieting with *ninacaspi*, I was feeling good so I decided I wanted to leave for Pucallpa. I rested for a day and then left. Unshaven with a long beard and long mustache, I arrived home. This time I stayed in Pucallpa for almost for a month, sculpting. The diets had given me good visions to work with, and I made some new pieces that I was able to sell. When I was away, my family would also sell any pieces that I'd made to support themselves.

During this time I could also have sex. The camphor I had used no longer affected my body, preventing me from having an erection. It loses its potency after a couple of months. If one uses camphor for too long, one may lose sexual desire.

One day, after about a month, I decided to return back to the jungle because I couldn't tolerate the noise and bustle of the city, and people always asking why I was so thin, pale-skinned, and unshaven. I looked a lot older.

My jungle encampment, which I had named Empire of Youth, was calling me. When I got there, I began a diet with *ucullu-cuycasha*. An *ucullucuy* is like a little gecko or *iguana*, and *casha* means spine. This tree, which grows along the riverbanks, is shaped like a *liana*, or a stick, has spines and a red sap, and is very bitter.

I drank the *ucullucuycasha* in the morning. Since this tree has spines, it was necessary to make contact with the sun when I drank it. Every tree that has spines belongs to the sun. They are solar plants.

The energy of the sun, transmitted through the plant, gave me the sensation that my body was burning. Rays of light seemed to come out through my eyes, and I also had visions of stars and colored lights. During the day my body was a little weak, my eyes were red, and I had to rest to be able to endure this plant. As the day progressed, I felt no hunger and had no desire to eat. Throughout the day not much happened besides the visions.

That evening I was unable to sleep and had visions all through the night, just like with *ayahuasca*. I felt like I was flying, and that a fire coming from the sun was burning me, and powerful rays were penetrating my body. Also it was as if I was being whipped, and surrounded by sharp teeth or spines. I was twisting and tossing in bed, and although I began feeling a little desperate, I had to endure what was going on because my vow was to live or die. I dieted with this plant for thirty days.

I was still having dreams of the beautiful, strange female spirit, Yara, who'd appear to me at night and when it was almost daybreak. She'd lie down with me, and I'd believe I was about to have sex, then awake to find she was just a spirit that had come, possibly to test me. For this reason I continued to use camphor to prevent erections and orgasms during the night.

I also had dreams of plants, in which new plants or trees were presented to me. Then the next day I'd go out to find those same plants that I'd dreamt about. In this way, I'd discover new plants and trees, which I would drink. I knew beforehand through Don Ramon, and through my grandfather and my cousin, Jacinto Tello, a great *brujo*, that it was necessary to try many different plants to become a shaman.

When I was about nine years old, I'd go to the farm with my cousin, Jacinto Tello. He'd pick up these small chilis, called *charapauchu*, which are extremely hot. He'd put a lot of them in his mouth, and they wouldn't burn him. I'd look at him and ask, "They don't burn you?"

"No, this is my *mullaca*," he'd say. *Mullaca* is a small sweet fruit. At that time I didn't know what a *brujo* was, or what a healer or a shaman did, but I knew that my cousin Jacinto Tello drank *ayahuasca*. He had cancer in his intestines, possibly because of too much chili, and too many diets. But he was considered a great *brujo*, and many feared him. I think he was addicted to *ayahuasca* and to the other plants that he'd drink, because he was always taking them.

After a month of dieting with *ucullucuycasha*, I didn't rest but started immediately to diet with *toé*, which is the *datura* plant. I'd heard my *maestros* say that one should drink a small quantity, about two spoonfuls, after boiling it. I put the resin, the core of the *toé*, in a cup, and the cup in the boiling water, and let it boil this way. When it was rubbery, I drank it directly without water. If prepared this way, it doesn't burn. The same method of preparation is used with *catahua*. These are the only two plants for dieting that are prepared in this way, using the *baño de maria* method. Opium is also prepared in a *baño de maria* method. Once I saw this Chinese man prepare opium from his garden. Using a toothpick, he'd remove the resin from balls on the flowers, and then put it in a *baño de maria*.

Toé gives one very strong, terrible hallucinations — much stronger ones than with *ayahuasca*, but different. Drinking *toé* can be dangerous, because it's the core of the tree that is drunk, and you can go mad or your neurons can be destroyed. Being alone, I had to observe my reactions to plants at the same time I was having visions — which was sometimes difficult.

Five minutes after I drank *toé*, my body started to jerk all over, with my arms twitching and jerking. I said to myself, "I'm not going to die, I will tolerate this." My head ached, and I began to see demons, colors, strange men, animals, and aggressive snakes that wanted to bite me. I tried to remain still but it was almost impossible. I told myself I needed to experience this. My body and my arms continued to move by themselves in all directions, but I forced myself to endure this intoxication which lasted all night.

This experience continued for three days, with the effects gradually weakening as the days went by. On the third day, though I was still feeling a little groggy and weak, I reassured myself, "My brain is strong, it hasn't burned my neurons, and I don't feel crazy."

Several days after drinking the *toé*, I dreamed about some fearsome black men who invited me to walk with them into the jungle. They took me to unknown places, where I had to cross over gorges, rivers and lakes, walking on the water. I felt like superman. Sometimes I flew, but my flights were heavy and I had no velocity. I saw things as if they were fantasies from the movies, such as the movie called *The Dragon Captive*. Carrying a big sword, I had a fight with a dragon and had to cross through a tunnel it guarded. These black men told me, "You need to defeat this animal or you'll remain here." My sword spouted fire, and when the dragon spewed fire at me, I'd cut at it with the sword. Eventually the dragon fell asleep, and then I walked over it's spiky back and through the tunnel. I came out of the tunnel, into a wonderful landscape, where the black men, no longer scary as they had been before, became like angels.

Other nights the medicine produced no visions. Then, after a few weeks, I dreamed it was storming, and I could see my children, who were crying and shouting. I saw my desperate wife, and I thought to myself that they must be having problems at home. I knew it was difficult for them, but I also knew they would have to endure this, as my decision was to learn, and I was learning.

All the first plant diets were for one month, until the entire cycle had been completed in a year. Then I started once again drinking the same plants, sometimes for more than two months. I then knew the plants from experience. All the medicines when used the first time are very strong, but afterwards one gets accustomed to them, and the body becomes strong. *Catahua* and *toé* are the two strongest plants. The effect of the plants is not instantaneous, but gradual, in preparation for the future. It takes five years to finish all the diets. The plants give strength and vigor to the body, as well as intuition, power, and energy to heal. From the moment you start drinking *ayahuasca* and dieting with *catahua* and *lupuna*, the mind and intuition start opening up. Just as food and vitamins are the body's allies, so plant medicines are a spiritual ally. They become an energetic companion in ones life. The body charges itself like a battery from the energies of each plant. Later these plants are transformed into one's bones, blood, cells full of energy, so you have the power to heal. This is what being an ally to the plants means. Plants also protect us from an attack by another *brujo*.

After experiencing the diets, people start considering one a *curandero* (healer). The first healing work is with children — those with fever, fear, or stress. This is because children more readily accept healers, and the healing is usually a positive experience. Thereafter, the reputation of a healer grows by word of mouth.

When I began healing, I'd blow tobacco on children, blowing crosses on their bodies. Or with *Agua Florida* (a perfumed flower water), I'd blow a fine spray, very powerfully and very fast, upwards from their feet. Not expecting this, the children would be startled and thus release their fear. Later I learned increasingly more ways to heal — it's an art.

After being on these diets for some time, it seemed incredible that each time after dieting and the fifteen days of rest, I had more vigor than before and the resolve to begin another diet. During the fifteen days between diets, I'd reflect well on what I'd experienced with the plant I had drunk.

Following my diet with *toé* I restored my body by eating everything. Then I traveled back to visit my family in Pucallpa. There I worked sculpting only with *renaco* roots. During that time I hardly slept, because many very beautiful ideas were coming to me from what I had seen in my visions — ideas related to social issues, such as poverty, misery, and the folklore of the Amazon. This time, I stayed at my home for a month to finish the sculptures,

which I needed to do before returning to the jungle to begin
dieting again.

After returning to my jungle encampment, I began the *chullachaqui caspi* diet. The *chullachaqui caspi* is not a very thick tree,
only about the width of the body, but it grows to about twenty
meters tall. Its roots grow about two meters high above the
ground, and they are like the tree's arms and feet. The tree is
strong, and pleasant to drink, and not dangerous. It has a very
bitter resin, but I was using the bark. No one had told me to drink
chullachaqui caspi, but, during the *toé* diet, in my visions I'd seen
the *chullachaqui caspi* trees. I was able to discover just by drinking
this plant that it was a medicinal tree. Later, after consulting with
other people, they confirmed to me that the *chullachaqui caspi* was
used medicinally.

There were many of these trees in the jungle, and I realized I'd
been using their roots to sculpt with, without knowing I was
wounding the tree.

About this time, the jungle near my encampment, Empire of
Youth, was being encroached on by a timber company, which was
exploiting the trees from this national park. I was suffering
because of the noisy machinery that was daily approaching closer
to my encampment. One day, before I had drunk the *chullachaqui
caspi*, I was walking along a path from my encampment, and
discovered they had knocked down some trees. I spoke to the
woodcutters in the timber company, asking them to please not
block my path because I always walked along that road. They said
okay, they wouldn't. But they still continued knocking down trees
at the rate of twenty or thirty a day. The animals screamed, the
birds shrieked, and the jaguars and deer escaped deeper into the
jungle. I remember recording the noise of hundreds of birds
shrieking, screaming, as they flew out of this area. The jungle
began sounding like a huge mechanical beast. I was in total
despair.

It was during this time that I was doing the *chullachaqui caspi*
diet. One day after scraping the bark with my machete and

collecting two handfuls of bark to soak in water, which I would then be able to drink the following morning, two strange men came into my encampment, saying they were lost in the jungle. I invited them to lunch, preparing plantains and meat that I had, but wouldn't eat during the diet. After eating, I showed them the way out, and returned to my encampment. It was about three in the afternoon, and I could still hear the machines going. I grabbed my drum and began to sing the *candil bandil* mantra while beating my drum. For about an hour, I sang and sang, and cried and cried, with all the feelings in my heart pouring out. I felt the timber people were going to expel me from there — the machines running over me and my encampment. There were already tourists and agents appearing. As I finished singing, a terrible storm developed, and it rained all night, covering the jungle floor with water.

The next morning I drank the *chullachaqui caspi*, but had absolutely no reaction. It was like drinking a glass of water, with only a slight prickling sensation in my throat, as though I lacked a little oxygen.

The rain continued all day long, and I couldn't go out into the jungle. I was working on my sculptures in a little hut when I dropped my chisel. As I went to pick it up, a spider jumped onto my hand and bit me between the thumb and the index finger. The spider grabbed onto my hand, and I had to shake it off onto the floor, where I could kill it. I crushed the spider after removing the head, and applied the ground spider to the bite. It had a couple of red dots on it's back indicating that it was dangerous. Since I had drunk the *chullachaqui caspi*, and it was raining heavily outside, I started to think that I could die of this spider bite. My arm began to hurt more and more, and then half my body became numb.

That night I began to write my will. I wrote down that my body was getting increasingly numb, and that if they ever found my bones it would mean that I had died from a spider bite and that nobody had killed me. I wrote that everything that was in my home was for my wife and children.

I couldn't sleep all night and felt a prickling, stinging sensation in my heart. At about five in the morning, I managed to fall asleep for a while. When I woke up at about nine that morning, I saw that my hand was very swollen. I put some *mapacho* (hand-rolled cigarette) tobacco in my mouth, chewed it, then swallowed the tobacco juice mixed with my saliva. Tobacco is a very different thing than *chullachaqui caspi*, and I felt a strong dizziness take me over. The next day I continued writing about my condition; that I was feeling better, that my hand wasn't that swollen, that the numbness was disappearing, that I probably wasn't going to die.

It continued raining and rained for a whole month, only stopping for a little while now and then. The machines that had created all the noise and destruction had been buried in the humid soil of the jungle because it rained so much. Through the drum playing and the *candil bandil* mantra, it seemed the spirits of the jungle had helped me. In addition, one of the administrators of this company, called Inforest, died. People said he had contracted tetanus through the steel cable from a tractor that had cut his body. Then the tractors stopped working because a new administrator came, and he also died of tetanus. Everything went wrong for the company.

Later it became known that this company belonged to a former president of Peru, who had allowed the exploitation of wood from this national forest. When I discovered they were going to divide the entire national park into allotments, I decided to request some land. They had already made a long path through the central part of this landscape, and were about to close me off from the other part.

Consequently, I went to an association of agriculturists, called Victor Raul Aria de la Torre, and paid about fifty *soles* to join the group. They gave me a lot, 250 meters wide and 2,800 meters long which was right in front of my encampment, but my intention was not to plant or do anything in this place. I had wanted it in order to protect myself from the encroachment that was taking place. It became apparent later that the goal of the association was to establish *coca* plantations, and a year later they began to do this.

The spider bite disappeared. I thought the spider had perhaps been part of the *chullachaqui caspi* spirit, or revenge the spirit of this plant had taken on me. If it was a punishment, I thought it was okay with me, because I'd now paid for having cut the root of this plant many times, before knowing about it. Once I knew the plant, I started to have a lot of respect for it, because in the *chullachaqui caspi* visions I'd meet with its spirit.

Although I began to know different plant spirits as I tried various diets, the principal one for me was the *chullachaqui caspi* spirit. In my dreams and visions I always encountered him, and he would invite me to his empire, where he had his house and where a *chullachaqui caspi* family lived. It was very beautiful to have known the empire of these spirits. It was like having lived with them. All of them loved me, and taught me about different medicines and healing methods. They told me, "When you're in danger, think of us, think of the tree, and think that you are united with us." These old spirits appeared to me like normal people, only smaller, with their heads wrapped up in colorful turbans. They were sitting, and I could see they were missing a foot and limped when they walked. They told me it was the only thing they didn't like about me, that I stared at their feet.

So I said to them, "But I like your foot. Probably you walk better with one foot."

They said, "Yes, we walk better, and we can jump better with one foot than with two."

I said, "You say it's nice to have only one foot. Why don't you cut mine off?"

"No, you have to die first, but you're needed here, and you're going to serve the people a lot."

During that time, I myself had seen visions of large groups of Americans and Europeans, without knowing that later on I would have considerable contact with people from the United States, Canada, and Europe. My diets took place from about 1971 to 1975. I started traveling in 1979.

At this point in my dieting I was very weak, had no strength to work, and always wanted to rest. So in this state I had many visions. According to the *maestros*, when you are bonded with the plant spirits, and drink them with respect, then you gain fortitude and acquire healing abilities.

Later, when I had quit dieting for about six months, I became very strong and powerful from all the knowledge I'd gained, and more capable of healing others.

One of my diets using a tobacco extract was almost lethal. This took place around 1961, before starting the five-year period of diets and before I had started working with Don Ramon. At that time I was having no luck because the animal traps I had set, using rifles that would go off when the animal entered the trap, weren't catching anything. At that time I was working as an electrician. Every day after work I'd go to place my traps. I found good paths, where the *majases* (huge nocturnal rodent) and *carachupas* (armadillos) would come and go, and I'd place the traps very well. During the night I would hear the rifles discharging, and the next day I'd go there expecting to find some animals. Up until then I'd always killed two or three animals using five weapons. I would place the weapon, connected to a thin string, on top of some sticks, and when an animal passed through, it touched the string and pulled the rifle's trigger. This is a well-known method of trapping in the Amazon.

With so much bad luck, I finally went to see a *maestro* Don Miguel Gatica, an old Bora Indian, and explained my situation. He said we should have some *ayahuasca* together, to see what the problem was. After drinking the *ayahuasca*, I didn't see anything related to my problem. I only saw animals, flowers, my work, my wife, and river trips. But Don Miguel saw that I had given away the head of an animal that I had killed. Some people who were jealous of me because I had been hunting well, used this head to harm me. Don Miguel explained to me they had harmed me by burying the head in some ashes to bring me bad luck.

When I asked him what I could do, he told me, "Well, tomorrow you should go to the cemetery at midnight by yourself. You need to walk around in the cemetery, without smoking tobacco. Being there will leave an impression on your mind, and you'll leave all your bad luck right there. Then, when you return, you are to remove your clothes outside the house, bathe yourself, and then go to sleep."

So the next night I remained awake until midnight, then left for the cemetery. Thinking that some spirit from one of the tombs could grab my legs, my body started trembling. Although I never experience fear, being in the cemetery so close to those tombs at midnight made it hard not to imagine all kinds of sinister things. It was a dark night and I could hardly see around me, but I was determined to stay for about an hour.

I stood on the tombs thinking about the dead people and what state their corpses where in, and prayed to receive good luck and to leave the bad luck there. Then, looking around, I saw some white forms, and my body trembled. I said to myself, "There's nothing that exists that can harm me. It's just fear." After about an hour, I returned home. On my way back, I looked behind me to see if any spirit was following, and I saw something chasing me. My body started shaking, and I was scared, but I continued on.

Removing my clothes outside the house as Don Miguel had told me, I heard whistles from spirits who were following me from the cemetery. I was afraid, but I had to bathe myself in the Ucayali River. Carrying a *paté* of *tutumu*, a tumbler made from half of a gourd, I went to the port and bathed in the canoe, fearing that a *Yacuruna* or a mermaid, or an alligator could be on the riverbank at that hour. Getting off the boat, I ran home, changed my clothes, and went to bed.

I believed in Don Miguel. He had told me that after doing this I was going to be lucky, but that I also needed to undergo the test of drinking tobacco.

That night I dreamed I had put up my traps, and that they had caught an enormous *majás* (large rodent-type animal).

The next day I went to see Don Miguel and told him I had done what he had told me to do. He asked me if I had been afraid. "A little," I said.

"You shouldn't have been afraid," he replied.

"But I was only afraid for a while. No spirit grabbed me. This afternoon I'm going to check my trap."

Near my trap there was a fallen plantain tree, and the *majases* were eating there — tasty animals whose meat is expensive. I heard a shot in the night, and very early in the morning I ran to the trap, expecting to find an enormous animal. Instead, I was surprised to find a small one-kilo *majás* cub that had strayed from its mother's side when it had gone to eat plantains. "This is better than nothing," I thought as I returned back with it. I went back to see Don Miguel and gave him half of the animal, after I had burnt off the hair in the fire. Soronjita and I made a good soup with the other half, even though it was small, together with peeled plantains.

That same day I placed another trap in the same spot, and that night I caught the large mother in the trap. I gave one leg to Don Miguel, who said I was now healed. He warned me not to give the head away, so that my enemies could not again put it in the ashes of the *tullpa* (the place where the food is prepared), and curse me.

Then Don Miguel told me we were going to the jungle the day after, and we would stay three or four days, adding, "I'm going to prepare a tobacco medicine. So go and get some tobacco."

"I have tobacco," I said.

"Then bring about two hundred grams of tobacco and we'll prepare it. We'll also look for a *remocaspi* tree in the jungle."

"I know where there's one," I said, "because I cured my father-in-law of a problem he had. He couldn't speak because he had a spell put on him, and I gave him this tree's bark and healed him." Don Miguel agreed we should go to the tree. It was a thick tree, about one meter in diameter, with protuberances on it. We looked for the best spot in the tree to place the tobacco after it was prepared. I had taken a small axe and some chisels with me, which I used to cut into the soft tissue of the tree to make the small space.

Don Miguel taught me how to boil the tobacco then filter it through a piece of cloth. Next we put the filtered liquid into a big cup, and placed it in the tree, covered with a fine gauze cloth. We then blocked up the hole with some of the splinters of wood that had fallen when we had cut into the tree, mixed with some mud.

He told me that in eight days we'd remove this medicine.

"Today we're making the *tambo*." This was a small open structure, which we constructed about three meters away from the tree. We also made a bed, like a platform made from the *huacrapona*, a palm tree which has spines. Once the *tambo* was ready, we made a covering to put on top to protect it from the rain. After finishing all of this, we returned home. There I told my wife that I was going to take a plant that would be a life or death test. Don Miguel had explained to me that if I survived after drinking this tobacco, then I could be a good healer.

Eight days passed by, and I wasn't afraid. Then Don Miguel came to my home and said, "Get ready. Prepare your mosquito net, your bed, and your sheets to take with you." It was about an hours walk into the jungle. I was anxious to drink the medicine, wanting to know what it was to experience death, or what it was to resist death. Arriving at the tree, we removed the splinters and the clay that were blocking the hole where the cup was, took the gauze off the cup, and observed how the tobacco was filled with growing spores and fermentation, so that it was actually moving. The cup of tobacco had received all the energy of the *remocaspi* tree over the eight days.

Don Miguel told me again, "This is life or death. Do you still want to drink it?"

"Yes, Don Miguel," I replied.

Then he sang his *icaros*, and with his *mapacho* (hand-rolled cigarette of jungle tobacco), blew the smoke over the cup of tobacco as a blessing. He stirred the mixture with his finger, and all the little spores moved. Finally, he asked me to drink it all. It was very bitter, and my body trembled. I wanted to vomit, but I resisted because I was not supposed to vomit. I stomped my feet and jumped, trying not to vomit. Don Miguel began to sing a *mariri*, dedicated to the tobacco. I started to feel incredibly dizzy and see black phantoms; the dizziness increased during the next ten or fifteen minutes.

When Don Miguel realized I was about to fall, he ordered me to get into the bed as fast as possible, and to not get out until I awakened, which could be at least three days.

In bed, I felt the earth spinning at top speed, and then, suddenly and abruptly, I felt nothing more. At nightfall, Don Miguel left me alone there, because in that jungle by Pucallpa there were no jaguars. I lay in the darkness in a semiconscious state, and I could see all of the landscape. I was a very tall man, more than twenty meters tall. The *remocaspi* tree was there, also huge, and I climbed onto its branches. Everything had multiplied in size. I sat in a yoga posture on top of the tree and saw huge black men who were so tall that even though they were standing on the ground they were as tall as where I was sitting. Their teeth were white and enormous, and when they sang their *mariris* it was so deafening that at first my ears couldn't receive the sounds. They were dark black Negroes, but their hair was long and straight like Indians, and their faces were sweet and pleasant, so I wasn't afraid. They kept on singing and singing. I remembered many of the tones and melodies of their music and later made up my own lyrics to them because I couldn't understand the dialect in which they sang. For a long time afterwards, these beautiful melodies and sounds stayed with me, and my head was always buzzing with this music.

In this vision, I also saw many animals, like enormous boas, who'd come and stand on the ground on their tails and whistle as if they were calling to other boas. These boas were winged and of many beautiful colors, and they would take off flying.

I stayed in this state of semiconsciousness for three days, without dying. After three days, Don Miguel Gatica returned. I'd been lying there without eating for three days, and Don Miguel brought a bowl of roasted plantain mashed up and mixed with hot water, which I drank since I was very weak. Although I was now in a conscious state, I was still having visions and could see spirits walking around. It seemed to me that I was in an unknown world where strange beings were walking and gathering plants, roots, and tree barks.

Finally Don Miguel said, "Let's return because it's late and getting dark. Can you walk?"

"Yes," I said, although I was weak. I was like a dog in love, who could hardly walk. I was pure bones, transparent and pale after drinking the toxic nicotine.

Don Miguel said, "Not many people survive this; many die, but you're fine. Now you'll be able to be a shaman and healer, if you want."

Tobacco is a powerful healing plant, as well as a protective spirit, and I use it all the time.

Once I met a man of the Shipibo tribe whose whole body was bleeding — his face, bald head, arms, legs — and he was dying. He was lying on plantain leaves, because if he'd been covered with a sheet, it would have stuck to his body.

I went and got about one kilo of tobacco, and brought it back to the Indians. We chopped it up and boiled it in about twenty liters of water. Then, with the tobacco liquid, I bathed the patient. The next day his skin was drier, and the bleeding was stopping. I bathed him three more times, and after the third wash the tobacco killed all the microbes on his body. He was healed only as a result of the tobacco. In hospitals they cannot heal such patients because they don't use tobacco, saliva, or urine.

During shamanic studies, we also try the different plants according to the visions that *ayahuasca* gives to us. *Ayahuasca* is a teacher who guides us, showing us very clearly which plants are important to drink. We can find these plants in the jungle because we have already seen them very clearly through *ayahuasca* the night before. Then a *maestro*, or the *ayahuasca*, can teach us how to go about preparing and drinking the plants.

For example if *ayahuasca* told us in a vision, or a teacher appeared in a vision, saying, "You need to drink *huayracaspi*," then immediately we search for the plant. It's better if you are told the name of the plant and not just shown what it looks like, because then you can go to a *maestro* and ask, "I want to drink *huayracaspi*, can you show me how?"

The teacher would then probably ask why, and you would

respond, "Because mother *ayahuasca* told me to take this plant."

The *huayracaspi* is a very tall, cylindrical tree, and it's bark is red and astringent. The teacher would prepare the *huayracaspi* for you. He would go to the jungle and remove a piece of bark from the side of the tree hit by the rising or setting sun. On the eastern side where the sun rises, the bark is thicker, and on the western side, it's thinner. That's why it's possible to orient oneself by using a tree when you gets lost in the jungle. When you completely peel off the bark, you can see the difference.

The teacher would then bring back the tree's bark, grind it, allowing about a hundred to two hundred grams for one person, and soak it overnight in a small amount of water. The next day he would strain the liquid through a cloth, blow his *icaros* into it, blessing it, and give it to you to drink.

A student doesn't necessarily work with a plant only once. If you're feeling weak in your journey or in your visions, you can drink the plants many times, after you've completed a five-year course of studies.

During the *huayracaspi* diet, there are almost no visions — only dreams of flying. *Huayra* means wind or air, while *caspi* is wood; so *huayracaspi* means "wind stick" or "air stick", a stick that makes us fly. You levitate and travel quickly or slowly. If you travel rapidly in your dream, it's because the *huayracaspi* is good. If it's very slow and you fall down at times, then you need to drink it again, and use a higher dose. *Huayracaspi* serves as a medium for spiritual travel, and for transmutation. To heal others, you can disappear and travel to Europe, to the United States, to China, to Japan, anywhere on earth. This ability to travel various places to heal is taught to us through this diet, through *ayahuasca*, or through the methods taught by other teachers.

There are incredible substances within the earth because the earth has everything within it — sweet, salt, colors, and poisons — it gives us the beauty of everything. There are many substances in the soil that give colors to leaves and flowers, that make plants grow, and that give taste to fruits and vegetables. This is why drinking clay or sand is beneficial to health. Boiled sand is very good for diarrhea, while boiled clay causes diarrhea. Interestingly, soil both stops diarrhea and stops constipation.

Murcuhuasca, a rope-like vine, has little balls within which are special substances that the sap deposits. These give the body strength and the ability to climb like Tarzan or a monkey that climbs up a vine to reach a treetop. *Murcuhuasca* is very powerful but very dangerous if you don't know how to diet with it. The diet is strict and lasts at least a month, preferably two. If a person drinks *murcuhuasca* they'll have no difficulty going wherever they want, even through vines, from tree to tree. While *huayracaspi* is used for flying, *murcuhuasca* is used to gain the ability to travel very rapidly through the jungle.

The *chuchuhuasha*, or *chuchuhuasi* as it's sometimes called, means astringent tree or gold tree, and prevents and cures rheumatism and protects against the cold. Fishermen, those who sail the rivers at night, or people who get wet a lot because their work is extracting gold or wood, should drink *chuchuhuasha*. If they don't they become pale and anemic. *Chuchuhuasha* balances the blood and warms up the body.

It's important for a shaman to drink *chuchuhuasha* because he travels physically and spiritually. Because shamans spiritually travel through the galaxies, visiting planets and cities to heal the ill, they have to go to cold places. When the spirit goes beyond an altitude of ten to fifteen thousand feet, it transmits a chilling cold to the body. Also, after drinking *ayahuasca*, one can feel this cold while traveling. The shaman needs to have strength, resistance to the cold, and energy. A shaman does these plant diets to become an exceptional person, unlike others who don't have the defenses to withstand a disease. While healing grave conditions like tuberculosis, AIDS, or other contagious diseases, generally the shaman doesn't receive these illnesses. As a shaman, I don't have time to get ill because I am constantly healing, or creating art, or building.

The *chuchuhuasha* that many people drink is mixed with rum and honey, but doesn't create an addiction to alcohol unless it is drunk in excess. One can drink *chuchuhuasha* without alcohol and honey, but it is much more bitter and astringent. A person who drinks *chuchuhuasha* is a healthy alcoholic, whereas an individual who drinks sugarcane alcohol is a sick alcoholic. Pure alcohol is not good. To be beneficial it should be mixed with some plant, like *chuchuhuasha*, *icoja*, *abuta*, or *ipururo*, which leave their healing substances in the body through the alcohol.

The diet with *chiriqsanango* is very delicate. *Chiriq* means cold, while *sanango* means that which heals the nerves. This plant which has multi-colored blue and white flowers, is poisonous if you drink from a very old, thick *chiriqsanango* plant. The root, the part which is used, should be only a half inch in diameter. One can drink from two roots, if there are problems with walking, due to chronic rheumatism, or when the feet are swollen from water or the cold, creating chronic rheumatism. Together with drinking the *chiriqsanango*, one needs to diet for a whole month, without salt, fruits, or other foods, only eating rice, plantains, and *boquichico*, a fish that doesn't have scales or teeth.

When a person drinks *chiriqsanango*, they don't feel cold, even if it rains, and are strong, healthy, pain free, and age slowly. If they immerse themselves in cold water, the water seems hot, and the body burns like fire.

Uchusanango (*uchu* means chili), is very similar to *chiriqsanango*; the diet is the same, and it's beneficial for the same conditions.

Achunisanango is also an important plant. *Achuni* is a little animal that weighs around five to seven kilos, with teeth that look like scissors and can slash a dog or person. When a dog wants to seize an *achuni*, many times the *achuni* destroys the dog's throat and kills him. According to tradition, when a man drinks a concoction of the ground up, bone-like penis of this animal, the man's sexual power never dies, even after he dies. Some people say that when men who drank the *achuni* penis died, their penis stayed erect, and when they were buried in a coffin, sometimes the coffin's lid was hard to nail down, and it was necessary to drill a hole in the coffin lid for the penis to stick out. I don't really believe this, and I've never seen it, but many people say it's true.

The *achunisanango*, whose root has nerve-like endings, is a substitute plant for the *achuni* penis. Drinking this root in alcohol with honey gives men sexual strength. I haven't met any homosexual shamans; the ones I've encountered have all been like Don Juan — with an excess of sexual energy and women.

Lorosanango is a plant used to treat diarrhea and give strength. *Loro* is a green bird, and the fruit of this tree is shaped like a bird's beak. The tree is about five meters tall, and has a very bitter bark. Although this plant is not native to Tamshiyacu, it can be grown here. Once that bark is dried and ground up into powder, it makes a very bitter powder that stops diarrhea. Shamans also drink this to strengthen the stomach and intestines, so that nothing can make them ill. In France, they have studied *lorosanango* and are making a medicine out of it called Donafan, for treating diarrhea.

Lobosanango is used to treat skin infections, called *carachas, sisos, psoriasis*. Lobo means wolf, and *lobosiso* is a psoriasis of the skin — the wolf disease.

There are many other plants that I've tried in my life. In the Amazon region, there is an almost endless variety of plants that may have potential for healing.

Chapter 16
Sculpting with Renaco Roots

After my first art exhibition in Lima in 1971, I continued exhibiting there up until 1974. With the help of the air force, I was able to travel back and forth numerous times from Pucallpa to Lima with my sculptures.

After one of my exhibitions in Lima, at the Instituto Nacional de Cultura, I met a woman who lived in Cuzco and fell in love with her. When I returned to Pucallpa, I told my family I was leaving for Cuzco to study stone carving. I ended up staying in Cuzco for three months. I purposely didn't give my family my address, so they couldn't find me if they came looking, but I received letters from them directed to the post office.

During that time, an American man came to Pucallpa trying to locate me, because he was looking for somebody to help him establish a lodge, a hotel for tourists. When he arrived in Peru, he immediately contacted Soronjita, because everyone had told him I was the only person who could help him. Then Soronjita wrote me asking me to come back to Pucallpa because there was an American man offering me work. In the meantime, the American and his wife had come to Cuzco to look for me. When I went to collect my mail, I found that this couple had been waiting for me for several days in the post office with a photo of me that Soronjita had given them. They called out my name, and when I acknowledged them, they came over happily and said "You're Agustin Rivas. We brought a letter from your wife, and this photo helped us to find you."

I went with them to their hotel to discuss their plan to open a lodge on Yarinacocha Lake at Pucallpa. I said that I could help them, by making the tables and chairs, and designing the lodge. Over the next three days I designed the lodge, and taking my designs, they left for the United States to have an architectural plan made.

Meanwhile, knowing they would return and had work for me, I went back to Pucallpa. By that time I was no longer seeing the woman I had fallen in love with because her mother didn't like me, and had made her life miserable because of it.

A month later, the Americans arrived in Pucallpa, and we went to the lake to look for some land. We found a tract that was very close to my workshop, on the same side of the lake. Subsequently, they began building the lodge.

I had already established an association of artists called New Eden, and with the money from the membership, I had gradually built eleven houses on my land for the artists to stay in. The American man, Nelson, became an honorary member, and one day I asked him if he would help to cultivate the entire five hectares of my land which ran along the lake for about half a kilometer.

Before Nelson had come to Pucallpa, I'd earned a lot of money through the many exhibitions that I'd had in Lima at places such as the French Alliance, the Raimondi College, the Italian Museum, the Peruvian Cultural Institute of North America, the Jesus Maria Library, and the Delfin Gallery. With this money I'd purchased some very nice land, where I had set up my studio. By the time Nelson had come, I'd already built a house, where I finished working on my sculptures.

Later, after Nelson's lodge was constructed, I also exhibited my sculptures there. He was a good friend, and every two or three months I repaired the furniture I had built for him, until later when his workers learned how to maintain it and I didn't do it anymore.

Soon tourists began staying at the lodge, and they'd admire my sculptures and the tables I'd made. Among them were beautiful women, who'd often fall in love with me because I was an artist, so I had the opportunity to experience romantic interludes with many women. My sculptures, all carved from the *renaco* roots, were phantasmagoric and reflected Amazonian mythology and folklore.

The characteristic of the *renaco* tree is that over hundreds of years it's roots join together, as if they are welded. According to Roger Rumrrill, as expressed in his poetry, these trees are joined together in an embrace of love. My sculptures were unique, called "Amazonian Apparitions" by Rumrril. I liked to work with *renaco* because the root forms seem like animals, humans, and mythological beings. I enjoyed gathering the roots and being in the jungle with these trees.

In 1976, I climbed a very tall *renaco* tree because about twenty meters (sixty feet) up there was a branch that had formed a cross shape with another branch. I was interested in this cross because I frequently created Christ figures. I've made about a hundred and fifty Christs for churches, cathedrals, and homes, and people love them.

I was sitting on this branch, with my legs wrapped around it, and cutting with my small motorized saw. Then I noticed that the other branch was actually coming from the tree next to the one that I was on. The branches had so much tension, due to the way they were joined that, when I cut the branch, it broke, hitting my legs violently and throwing me upwards. I flew about eight meters (twenty-six feet) in the air, before falling rapidly. I was like an agile cat, and I grabbed onto a *catahua* tree that was there. *Catahua* trees have spines, as hard as nails, all the way down their trunks, with a resin that burns.

Hugging the *catahua*, I slid down about four or five meters (fifteen feet) at a great speed. As a result, my arms and my chest were torn open. Luckily I was wearing clothes, but my shirt had short sleeves. When I made it down to the ground, I saw that my arms were very injured. Although I hadn't fractured my bones, the nerves in my right arm had been pulled out, and I was bleeding badly. Alone there, I knew I had to get myself back to my encampment. So I took off my shirt, tore it in half, wrapped up my arms, and walked back to my workshop, which was not too far away.

At first I didn't go to the hospital because I didn't want them to amputate my arm. I was afraid and I thought it was better to heal myself at home. Instead I unwrapped my blood-soaked shirt from my arms, and saw that my nerves had been pulled out. I used a pair of scissors to cut the hanging nerves. My fingers had shrunk on both arms, especially on my right arm. Next I boiled tobacco and washed my arms with it and then applied *permanganato* a pharmaceutical preparation, mixed with hot water. In this way I cured my arms. Afterwards I poured a red antiseptic liquid from the pharmacy onto them and wrapped them with gauze.

After the accident, everything dried up really well, but my fingers were still shrunken, and I had no sensation in them. However, I kept saying to myself, "I'm going to recover." In a month I was healed, but I had terrible scars on my arms from the accident. Then I spoke with a doctor I knew, and asked him to get me some human fat. I'd been told that human fat could get rid of the scars from accidents. He was able to get me some from an autopsy that he'd performed on a person who had died in an accident. I dissolved this fat in a small pot and added some perfume to change the odor. It smelled like pig fat; and it reminded me that I had eaten human flesh, so it didn't seem unpleasant to put human fat on my arms. Little by little, this fat did get rid of the scars until they had almost entirely disappeared. It was amazing to see how my skin could be regenerated so quickly — no doubt due in part to the fact that I didn't drink alcohol, I had a simple diet, and had used many plant medicines to strengthen my body.

In about 1978, a plant called *huama* started growing on the lake. It was very dangerous, and people couldn't travel by boat. The students and farmers could not go to the Yarinacocha port by Pucallpa, because there was too much *huama*. The lake of Yarinacocha had two points, one on the east and the other on the north. The winds would always come from the east, so the plants would accumulate on the north side, in the port. Thus the boats could neither come nor go, and students couldn't get across the lake.

As a result, I had problems with Nelson, who went to the United States and brought back some of the chemical called Agent Orange, which he wanted to use to eradicate this plant. But in the meantime a multisectorial committee had been formed to solve the problem with the mayor of Yarinacocha a member. They discussed the Agent Orange with Nelson, who wanted to charge twenty million *soles* to use this substance.

As an alternative way of dealing with the plant, I invented a machine which was a flat boat with a motor, on top of which were placed twenty-five hand disk saws used to cut wood. They were two inches apart, with rotating edges that would make cuts of about a one inch width each. The blades were fifteen inches in diameter, and would go seven inches into the water, destroying the plant from its root.

It was an ingenious device that I knew would work. So I contacted Nelson and showed him my design. I'd also gone to a mechanical engineer to have it approved. The engineer told me that where the motor was located in the boat I needed to put some metal rods that would detect wood inside the *huama* and prevent it from colliding with the saw blades. I asked him if he could do this, and he said he could for six million *soles*. At that time millions of *soles* was not a lot. I had also decided to have the design approved by Sinamos, a state organization.

However, when I showed Nelson my design, he became very angry and he almost hit me.

"What's wrong?" I said. "This is going to be beneficial for all the people."

"I have a better way of taking care of the problem!" he yelled.

"What's your way?" I asked him.

"You wait and see!" he responded.

I began to talk to the people who belonged to the multisectorial committee, who told me that it was the Agent Orange, which had been used in Vietnam and had been found dangerous for the land, fish, animals, and people. I then consulted with a German doctor who said, "It is very dangerous." There was an ecologist and biologist, Juan Panai, there too, and he couldn't believe the American planned to use the dangerous substance.

They began to make inquiries about whether Agent Orange was indeed about to be used. I myself saw a man from Nelson's multisectorial committee pouring some onto the plants by the edge of the lake, which burned them. They were planning to fumigate by air with an airplane, to make the plants rot and sink into the lake. But in the process they were going to ruin the whole lake, killing the insects, birds, and fish; the entire ecological balance of the lake was going to be destroyed, and people would not be able to bathe in the lake or drink its water, creating a human catastrophe.

The next morning I went to the lake and hired people to work for me, agreeing to pay any price they asked. About a hundred people gathered to work and remove the *huama*.

When we started to remove the plants, Nelson came over very angry and said, "Who gave you the order to work on this?"

"I did," I said, "because you're not going to throw Agent Orange in here."

"Yes, I will!" he asserted.

"No, you won't. The people know already that you cannot do anything here. Go and do it in your own country and see if they'll let you do it!" I shouted. As a result of the dispute, he became my enemy.

We removed about a hundred tons of *huama*, but every day there was more and more of it. Then a company of ecologists started using a net, pulled by two motorboats, one on each side, at the northern side of the lake where there was a pipe that drained into the Ucayali River. In this way we were able to completely remove the *huama*.

Nelson didn't get to use the Agent Orange, and he lost money, which he had intended to use to build more bungalows.

The newspapers wrote stories about the disagreement between me and the American. Although, he was mad at me, he hadn't thrown my sculptures out of his lodge. So one day when only his wife was there, I went to retrieve them.

Nelson was also starting to cut wood in my territory to build bridges. He'd made a road approved by the municipality, so that he could go by car to his lodge. But previously we had signed a document at the police station agreeing that there would be no road. So I denounced him to the police for cutting down a tree, and he was obliged to pay half a million *soles* to the forestry service. He didn't want to pay because he was influential. So I went to Lima to talk to my friend Roger, who was the public relations director for the Agricultural Ministry. Ultimately, Roger made the American pay half a million *soles* for cutting down one tree.

One day, a few weeks later, I heard him cutting down another tree. I immediately went to the site and saw that with a motorized saw his workers were cutting down an ancient hundred-year-old mango tree that always produced fruit eaten by the locals. By the time I made it there, the tree was already cut in half, and it had to be cut completely to prevent it from falling.

After this I went to the forestry police and brought three policemen with me to see the American. They went to his lodge, while I waited for them. They returned happy, and it appeared that Nelson had given them whiskey or money. They told me the tree had bothered the American because he had trouble driving underneath it, and it was producing too much shade. I demanded to know why this man had cut a tree on my legal property and said he had no right to do so. Their response was, "Well, he's a foreigner, and it's better not to mess around with him."

"Well, he's not going to get away with it." I said.

Some time later Nelson passed by in his car while I was working in my workshop, which was two or three meters away from his road. Each time he'd pass by my house he'd accelerate his car and stick his tongue out at me like a child. He'd also removed the muffler to annoy me, causing his car to make an intolerable roaring sound. I grabbed my bow and arrow, and out of anger, I shot an arrow into the air. It was an arrow I used for practice that didn't have a point, but only a little ball.

There was a Shipibo Indian woman riding along in the car, who saw me shoot the arrow. She told the American that I was shooting at him. He put his car in reverse, jumped out, and came towards me like a beast, ready to hit me. With a small axe in my hand I warned him not to hit me. He wanted to grab the bow to show to the police, as proof that I was threatening him. I said, "If you take my bow from me, I'm going to cut your car's tires with my axe. Finally, he left.

A few days later he came looking for me at my home, saying that some tourists needed me. He acted as though he had forgotten everything that had taken place. I told him, "I believe that you're half crazy, and this is dangerous. You lost control because you believed an Indian woman telling you that I was shooting at you."

"Okay, let's forget it." he answered. "I only want you to take care of these tourists and explain to them how you make your things."

Later Nelson did something that seemed even crazier. He bought an entire town, with all its people and a school, which was included in the purchase of the land, as well as the name of the town. Since the board of the municipality was his ally, and the mayor was his friend, when people denounced what he'd done, the mayor did nothing. He could bribe everyone with his money except me.

Then around 1987, Yarinacocha became the focus of terrorism. At that time, nine out of every ten people were terrorists. I found out that the lodge was being destroyed, and in two days there wasn't even a stick left. The workers who had been employed by Nelson, had taken everything because he hadn't paid their salaries before leaving for the United States.

Chapter 17
International Travel and New Eden

In 1979 I began traveling much more than I had in the past. By this time my arms were functional, although without sensation. Nevertheless, I continued to sculpt, but with some difficulty, and began to travel more than sculpt. In 1979, at the invitation of the German government, I traveled to Germany to exhibit my sculptures at the Peruvian Consulate in Hamburg.

In Germany, I contacted a doctor, Dieter Ludicker, whom I'd met in Cuzco, and he came to my exhibition at the consulate, which began July 27, 1979. Diplomats from many countries attended, and every day I'd be at the gallery to explain my art to visitors, be photographed for the newspapers, and plan the next day's itinerary. Every day we'd visit museums and other tourist attractions in Hamburg, accompanied by a retinue of representatives of the Red Cross, television networks, or reporters from newspapers. I had interviews with journalists, and visited writers and other artists.

One day when Dieter Ludicker invited me to have a meal with him, he saw the problem that I had with my arms and said, "I have a friend who can look at your arms. He's a surgeon at the Ependorf University in Hamburg. We need to see him." Dieter Ludicker was a surgeon who also worked at the university and operated on patients with pituitary cancer.

His friend, Dr. Roland Mücke, received me warmly since I was a guest of the government and an artist who needed help. He agreed to operate on me free of charge, and I was very happy he would help me. He analyzed my arms with a machine. The needle of the machine didn't move, showing that my nerves weren't functioning. Working with the resulting analysis, he opened my arm with a cut about forty centimeters long and worked for about six hours. I was awake during the whole procedure but had a strange reaction from the local anesthesia. First, I cried and cried. There was a female nurse standing at my head, and Manfred, another friend from Germany, was at my feet, because he spoke Spanish and could translate. Because of her white mask I could only see this woman's eyes, and said, "What beautiful eyes you have. I'm in love with your eyes. I'm sure that your body must be gorgeous, too." She asked Manfred what I was saying, and when he interpreted, everyone started laughing and saying, "He's an artist, like Picasso and Dali." Then I also started laughing and laughing. All my emotions were coming out, probably stimulated by the anesthesia. At the same time I knew the doctors were repairing my arm, and I was feeling so much happiness that they were helping me. As they worked, I could feel the nerves from my right arm going into my chest, but there wasn't any pain. After six hours, I could feel each stitch as they sewed me up, and then placed my arm in a black sling. Afterwards my arm functioned better, although, to this day, I still have no sensation in my hands.

While in Germany, I also visited a pretty German woman I had had a relationship with in Yarinacocha. She had stayed with me there for a month. We exchanged letters for two years, but I never thought that I'd be going to Germany so eventually I stopped writing. Then, when I was in Germany, she came to see me and invited me to stay at her home. However, by that time she was already engaged to be married, so our romance didn't continue.

After visiting her, I returned to Ependorf University to have my hand operated on. The other cut was almost healed. This time they cut from the heel of my hand to my wrist, and then to my baby finger. The five-hour operation was extremely painful, even with the anesthesia.

A month later the German government sent me a letter reminding me I had to go back to Peru, which I did on August 27, the day before my birthday on August 28. My arm was still in a sling, as the wrist had to heal. My friend Roger was waiting for me at the airport in Lima, with some reporters who interviewed me. Then I went to Pucallpa, where my return from Germany was big news on the radio and among my friends.

I hadn't sold anything while in Germany, as everything that had been exhibited there had been purchased before I left Pucallpa. With this money I'd bought the land where we were living, but had been paying rent for the house. I bought the land with the intention of eventually building a new and bigger house.

A year later, on August 30, 1980, right after my birthday, there was a fire at my house, and everything in it was completely burned, including my tools. Nobody knows how the fire started, but I suspect a tenant of mine, with whom I was having problems, caused it. I'd sued this man because I was trying to evict him, and he didn't want to leave. It took six years for the case to be resolved. Eventually I won the trial, and he had to move out — the verdict was given shortly before my house burned down.

The fire completely destroyed everything, but fortunately, nobody was hurt except my dog who got trapped. As a result, my whole family was left with only what they'd been sleeping in, and I was left with only my underpants. From the moment I was left with nothing, I had to think positively, rather than devoting myself to alcohol, like many others do after losing their belongings. Afterwards institutions and people we knew gave us clothes, household items, and shelter. In addition to donations of goods, the Rotary Club organized a fundraiser for me, but some people objected to giving me the money, suggesting instead that it be given to other people who were in worse situations.

I started to rebuild immediately, but since I had no documents and no property titles, I had to have all the paperwork done again. It took me the next five years to rebuild my house, and as a result, I couldn't travel for a while. While my family stayed in the house of a friend, I returned to the burned house, and started to work and live there.

Eventually a German woman, who worked for German television at the embassy, came to film the state of my house, and the German embassy gave me money to help out with the reconstruction.

When the filmmaker and I went to the jungle where I collected *renaco* roots, because she'd been wanting to document where I got the wood for my sculptures, we both fell in love with each other, took off our clothes and made love. Although the mosquitoes were biting us all over our bodies, she didn't mind.

After the fire I wandered around Yarinacocha with my machete getting what wood I could. I managed to get a saw and began working at the house site. I had to put all the debris from the fire in piles in the street with the help of friends and family. There was no water, no electricity, nothing. I closed the front of the house with burnt *calaminas*, the metal corrugated roofing. I had nothing, so I had to use what I could.

I had 20,000 *soles* in savings — 20,000 *soles* was like 2,000 *soles* now — which I withdrew from the bank to buy bricks and cement. I made a brick wall in the front of the house to protect everything from thieves. Then I worked inside. Friends who worked at the San Juan Beer company also helped. It was difficult because some of my tools had no handles, and others were useless. Later a woman gave me a wood plane, and I started to work with it. I put up four of the burnt *calaminas* to protect myself from the sun, because in the morning the sun was strong.

To earn more money to continue reconstruction on the house, I turned to my art. I found a root to carve that looked exactly like a dog and carved it to look similar to my burned pet. Because I did this devotionally and with all of my inspiration, it was a beautiful dog. It saddened me to sell it, but I needed money to continue the house. I sold it for about 15,000 *soles*, and, with this money, I built another brick wall on the right side of my house. On the back side there was a wall belonging to my neighbor, and on the left side there was another low wall, belonging to the house next door. Because it was low, I asked permission from the owners to add another one and a half meters of wall. After I had the four walls, I was protected and had more privacy. Although the help we received after the fire did not solve all our problems, we began to reconstruct the house and recover the family prestige.

I continued sculpting, experimenting with new discoveries in my art. One day I went to look for *renaco* roots, having borrowed a motorized saw. I was cutting roots when somebody called my name. There was no one around, and I knew immediately that it was the *renaco* spirit calling me, making me aware that I was hurting these trees by cutting their roots.

So I spoke to the spirit saying, "I want to give you life and form. I want you to last longer. If you stay here, you'll die rotting. But if I transform you into sculpture you'll live much longer and people will admire your new form." Then I asked forgiveness from the spirit for cutting the roots, which would result in killing some of the trees. The *renaco* tree can regenerate quickly because it has many roots connecting with other plants, but, no doubt, I did kill some trees by cutting roots.

For me the interaction between my art and plant medicines was very important. Without the plant medicines, I couldn't have made the sculptures; and without experiencing the *ayahuasca* ceremonies with Don Ramon, I wouldn't have been able to visualize the many phantasmagoric and mythological forms of my sculptures. My works reflected Amazon mythology as well as local society, including laundry women, water men, musicians, and woodcutters.

About a year later, I got an idea to establish a retreat for artists in a quiet and secluded area. In the search for a possible place, I went to the Boqueron of Padre Abat, about two hundred kilometers from Pucallpa, where there were tall mountains, the Aguaytia River, and a big bridge. I climbed the nearest mountain, where there was a waterfall called the Bride's Veil. It was a beautiful place, and I decided to sleep there one night. The people from Boqueron were afraid to go there, saying that a chained woman wandered around there, intercepting trucks when they passed by. If they saw this chained woman, the trucks would drive by rapidly, without stopping. The story didn't scare me but only made me curious about whether it was true.

Afterwards I returned to Pucallpa, where I prepared wood and some *calaminas* (corrugated metal roofing) to take back to the mountain. I cut everything to the right measurements for building a house. A close friend of mine, Guillermo, was a businessman who sold soft drinks and made deliveries to the area. I told him that I wanted to build a small house in the Boqueron and asked him to take me there in his truck.

After he agreed, we left, along with a good friend, Alfredo, who'd frequently come to my house to paint in solitude.

When we got there, Alfredo told me he liked the place but that it was very dangerous.

"What danger can there be here?" I said. "This is a pretty place, let's build the retreat for artists here."

"Very well," he said, but he went back that very same day, leaving me alone with my materials.

To build the little house, I had to climb up by myself, carrying the materials. Up where the Bride's Veil started, there was a very small flat area and the abyss. At the bottom of the abyss there were some trees, their tops level with where I was. With the boards that I had brought with me, I made a floor and some side supports, and began to build a roof with *calaminas*.

After working the rest of the day, I ate a meal, then hung up my hammock and went to sleep happy. I awoke at dawn to the song of very pretty yellow birds with crests, that looked like little colorful parrots. They are called rock roosters. Up that high there weren't any mosquitoes, only little bees that flew into my eyes constantly.

When the little house was finished, I went back to Pucallpa to get groceries, tobacco, my rifle, and a pair of glasses to protect myself from the small bees.

During the day I'd climb the mountain looking for colorful pieces of wood. There were bears there, but they never attacked me. Instead, they'd jump into the abyss when they saw me. They wouldn't die, and later I'd see them rolling on the ground.

Thinking that there might be a lake further in, I began to explore the area. Eventually, I came to the little flat area where the water was running that formed the waterfall. For a day, I kept on walking without discovering a lake, only finding magnificent pools of pure green and blue water, which were wonderful to bathe in and drink.

In the pools I found stones so soft that I would leave tooth marks when I bit into them. They were great to sculpt with, but, when they dried they became hard and were impossible to work on, so they had to be worked with quickly, to make use of their softness. I started to carve these stones, using my wood carving tools, then sold them for two or three hundred *soles* each.

Later, I worked on a stone wall, part of the mountain that was soft because of dampness. On the wall I carved the words "New Eden," the name of my retreat for artists. There I spent days, eating plantains and *fariña*, but I didn't drink *ayahuasca*.

One night there were many glow worms flying around, and I began to gather them in a box. There were so many of them that night that I could light my whole space with their green light. I put them in a transparent plastic bag, until the bag looked like a brightly lit bulb. Gathering glow worms in the night, playing my harmonica, lying in my hammock, and falling asleep to the soothing sound of the Bride's Veil, I felt like I was in a paradise.

One night I awoke at eleven to a ferocious storm. It was thundering and lightning, with terrible electric discharges. It felt as though lightning was striking the peaks of the Cordillera Azul, and there were big rocks falling into the ravine of the Bride's Veil, where I was. There was a crescendo of sounds. The tempest grew stronger, and it started raining even harder, with the thunder and lightning bolts increasing. I was scared because water from the Bride's Veil had turned into a huge river and was approaching me. I could already see particles of water coming into my small house. I quickly got all my necessities together and left the house. Just a moment afterwards something hit the house with a loud crash, and carried it away with everything in it, into the abyss where the waterfall was crashing down, a fall of about eight hundred meters. I had escaped dying in that place by just thirty seconds.

The next day at dawn the tempest was still raging. I tied my bag up with a rope, then tied a pole onto a rock so that I could use the pole to climb down to the road. Wet and muddy, I managed to make it to the highway and the narrow Yurak River, which was spanned by a bridge. The water was almost up to the level of the bridge, and after crossing it, I came to a guard house situated there because a tunnel was in the process of being built. When I went over to it to ask for refuge, a man pointed a rifle at me intending to shoot because he thought that I was a demon. I told him, "I'm a person. I was living up there!"

But he answered, "No, there's a demon up there. If you were living up there, then you're the demon. Get out of here!" and he threw me out.

Disconsolate, I started to walk towards Pucallpa. About one kilometer away where a hostel was under construction, a worker recognized me. I told him how I had escaped falling into the Bride's Veil and how I was saved by a miracle. He was amazed, and told me to come with him to rest and eat. I changed into dry clothes from my bag which had kept them dry because it was plastic, and then waited while he prepared a rooster that he caught. After eating, I felt strong again.

Then we went for a walk towards the mountains hunting for a deer or other food. Due to the rain, there were mountain slides everywhere, and the Yurak River was roaring, with the sound of boulders rolling around with the force of it's current. This was a typical flood that occurs once a year in that region. Nobody can live there during that time.

The man then suggested crossing the Yurak River to where there might be papayas and bananas. However, the water currents had changed everything, taking away trees, bridges, and roads, and making it impossible to cross. So we returned to his house, and I slept there that night.

The next day we went to see what had happened at New Eden, and there was nothing left of the house. Even larger boulders near the Bride's Veil had been moved. Once again I was thankful I had survived.

I returned to Pucallpa disappointed my project hadn't worked out. However, after I told some artist friends what had happened, they agreed to go back to the area with me and look for a better location higher up beyond the Bride's Veil.

We took the bus to Lima and got out at the Boqueron del Padre Abat. The Boqueron was a very dangerous area, a canyon between Pucallpa and Lima and Huanuco or Tingo Maria. The place got its name in 1920 when Father Abat wrote it on a mountain wall, probably hanging over the mountainside with ropes to do it.

We discovered a path very high up, but it was very dangerous, and we had to tie ropes above to assist our climb. The most agile member of our group had to go up first to tie the rope, so the rest of us could carry the loads of supplies we'd brought.

Soon we discovered a beautiful place to build another house, but the lightning was still dangerous in that area. This region, where the Amazonian plain started, was called the "eyebrow of the jungle."

We spent two nights there, explored the area, and then returned back to Pucallpa without incident. However, a week later when we came back, I had another near accident. On the way up, at the top of the Bride's Veil, there was a very dangerous path. Because I was the strongest, I was carrying food, a rifle, and a bag in which I carried four bottles of *pisco*, a strong liquor made of grapes.

Jorge and Guillermo were already up above, and they had tied the rope to a tree hugging a rock with its roots. When I began to climb up, suddenly a stone broke loose and left me hanging, with the abyss about a hundred meters below me. I hurt my arms again in the same place as before; my hand was bloody, and I thought I was going to die there. My rifle was hanging in one direction, and the bag with the bottles in another direction. The belt that was around my forehead, supporting the big bag, had dropped down to my neck and was almost strangling me. I had to use all my strength to shift it away from my neck and onto my shoulders. My friends were pulling on the rope because the little tree was about to break loose from the rock. Ultimately, they had to support the rope all night long.

It was raining, windy, and cold. I stuck my hand in the bag, pulled out a bottle of *pisco*, and drank it, then threw the bottle into the abyss. The wind was howling, the trees were blowing, and a cloud of fog covered the whole area so that I couldn't see anything. After drinking the bottle of *pisco* I felt less cold and desperate. In the end, I finished up all the four bottles of *pisco*. I was feeling dizzy and my body was numb due to the alcohol, so I didn't feel cold and fell asleep hanging, leaning my head on the rope.

It was an impossible situation with the way I was hanging. There was a boulder above my head blocking my view of the others, so I couldn't see them, and they couldn't see me. Just before dawn, I woke up and suddenly saw a head looking down at me, saying, "Aguchito, are you okay?"

Then a rope was thrown down to me, and I tied it to the big bag, which they managed to pull up. After they pulled up the rifle and the bag which had held the *pisco*, they began pulling me up. I struggled to make it to the edge of the boulder that was overhead, and finally managed to climb up on to it.

The food supplies and clothes were soaked, and I told them we should return.

So, about 8:00 A.M. we started to descend very carefully. When we made it to the trail above the highway, two cars came by, but when the drivers saw us they got scared and refused to give us a ride. Our faces were distorted from the troubling night, and we must have looked like demons, drug traffickers, or terrorists.

Then I said, "I'm going to lie on the road, so the next car will have to stop." This worked, and the driver got out of the car and asked what had happened. My friends said that I had had an accident, and we wanted to go to Aguaytia. He agreed to give us a ride and left us at the customs-control shack.

My uncle, who was the chief of customs, was there together with one of his co-workers. I told him about our ordeal, and they cleaned and bandaged my arm and gave us breakfast.

It was about 11:00 in the morning, and a bus from Lima arrived. I asked my uncle to tell the bus driver to take us to Pucallpa, but he refused, saying the bus was full. The driver thought we didn't have money to pay the ticket, and that my uncle was asking them for free service. So I asked the driver the fare, and paid it.

Some acquaintances of mine from Pucallpa on the bus asked me what I was doing there, and I told them I was exploring the area to build a retreat where artists could come to create artwork. Because Pucallpa was so crowded and noisy, I told them it was not possible to work there. When we arrived in Pucallpa, I had to go to have my arms healed.

Fifteen days later we went back to the area, because it was so beautiful and peaceful. A policeman was on the bus with us, and he asked me where we were going. "To the Boqueron, because I want to build an encampment there," I answered.

"That area is dangerous. Do you know that there are drug traffickers there?" he replied. "Be careful, they can kill you. They pass through there, evading the customs control."

Despite the warning, we climbed up again, having found another less dangerous path. This time the weather was good, and we were happy. On the way to the mountaintop, we saw footprints and marks where people had pulled something along the trail. I said, "The drug traffickers have come this way."

So we waited for almost two hours until we heard voices below. Hiding, we watched them pull up sacks of drugs. They went up, and then came back down and left. Luckily they didn't go to where our tents had been located.

We realized that we couldn't come back anymore.

Since I couldn't establish a retreat in the Boqueron of Father Abat, in 1985 I founded an artists association called New Eden in Yarinacocha. At around that same time, I began to participate in more *ayahuasca* ceremonies with Don Ramon, establishing a stronger alliance with him and assisting him when necessary.

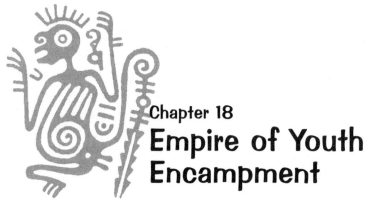

Chapter 18
Empire of Youth Encampment

One day a group of Americans arrived with a man who was bringing groups to Peru to do spiritual work. Another Peruvian shaman from the coastal area near Lima, Don Eduardo Calderon, was also traveling with them. They stayed at the lodge in Yarinacocha, and after seeing my sculptures, wanted to meet me.

During this encounter we began to converse about which shamans lived in Pucallpa. The man, Arimuya, who was the group's leader, asked me if I knew of an *ayahuasquero* shaman.

At that time I wasn't strongly established in my work, since I felt I still didn't have enough experience with *ayahuasca*. So I told him I knew an old shaman named Don Ramon Sanchez Rojas, who was very good.

Arimuya wanted to meet Don Ramon, so we went to his house. After I introduced him to Don Ramon, Arimuya told him, "Don Ramon, I am with a tourist group of about forty people, who want to drink *ayahuasca*. Agustin tells me he has a camp far from town, and we would like to go there, but first we would like to do an *ayahuasca* ceremony here in Yarinacocha. We want to see how you work."

"Very well," Don Ramon said, "it would be a pleasure to help you."

Then Arimuya invited Don Ramon and myself to lunch at the lodge, Don Ramon agreed to do a ceremony there the next day. Don Ramon asked for 3,000 *soles*, which is equivalent to 500 *soles* now. I asked nothing for myself because I was Don Ramon's assistant.

The next day, Arimuya came to my house to reconfirm everything. Then we picked up Don Ramon and headed for the lodge. At nightfall we did the ceremony on a platform at the lake's shore. Don Ramon served the *ayahuasca*, and I assisted him.

This ceremony was the first one for so many people, and I also felt, for the first time, like a *maestro*. I had a *vara* (a magical wand), made of *pijuayo*, a palm tree six to seven inches in diameter. Inside the palm there is a soft pulp, but around the contour, the thickness is about an inch and very hard and black. If the tree is struck by lightning, it receives an electrical charge and splits open. From these pieces *varas* are made, which still hold the electrical energy. Such a wand has a very positive effect in magic.

After we drank the *ayahuasca*, Don Ramon began to sing. In the ensuing wonderful state of consciousness, I began to see very beautiful visions, lights, and landscapes. All the people vomited and cried, because *ayahuasca* takes out all ones bad experiences, all stress, all traumas, and all diseases from the body and the soul. I helped Don Ramon with the blowing of tobacco to cleanse the area, and afterwards to purify and heal the people.

The next day we had a meeting with the participants so they could process and understand their experiences, just as I do today. Because Don Ramon had never had the experience of discussing participant's experiences of the *ayahuasca* before, he answered questions harshly, and many of the people there misunderstood and were upset and resentful. For example, when they asked him why they had vomited, instead of giving a technical explanation Don Ramon answered brusquely, "Your stomach is full of shit," or "You must have intestinal worms," or "These are things that don't interest me. It's your problem to figure out why you have vomited so much." As a result, some people complained to me. I explained that Don Ramon was a good shaman, but not accustomed to discussing the experience of ceremonies.

The next day the group, Don Ramon and I went to the jungle, to the encampment I had named Youth Empire, as requested by Arimuya. I had called my encampment Empire of Youth, because it was there that my life had been rejuvenated. I studied and became a shaman there, spending five years in that tree undergoing all my diets with plants.

We hired a big bus, and cooks from the lodge, and on the way found porters to carry all the supplies. When the bus arrived at the 67 kilometer sign, which marked the way in to my site, we got off and began our walk into the jungle. It was an adventure with so many people. At one point we had to cross a river in a fragile canoe that only held two people at a time, but we all crossed without incident.

On the other side of the river we met an old Indian woman and her husband, whom I hired to go with us into the jungle to be in charge of hunting animal meat, primarily monkey. Later it turned out that the American group didn't want to eat monkey, so we gave them just the broth which was very delicious without the meat.

It was a ten-kilometer walk through the jungle to my encampment, and we needed a person with a machete to go ahead, cutting a path. I didn't go there often, and the jungle grows rapidly and abundantly. It was difficult for Don Ramon to walk because he was so old. By the time we were halfway there, Don Ramon was very tired and couldn't walk anymore, so we had to rest before continuing. Finally we arrived at my camp.

This place that I'd built close to the *shiwahuaco* tree was a paradise. There you could hear the jaguars roaring, along with other animals. There were *papagallos*, large parrots with long tails of blue, red and yellow, and many other birds. The houses that I had there served for sleeping and for preparing the *ayahuasca* in the rainy season.

This was the first of many groups Arimuya brought to my encampment over a period of about three years. He'd usually bring a group once or twice a year. After the first couple of times, Don Ramon stopped coming since the walk into the jungle was too difficult for him. Also the people that came with Arimuya said they preferred the way I worked with them. After a while, some of the people that had come on a regular basis started bringing their own groups, and in this way other groups were formed. This is how my work with people from other countries started to expand.

The next night, under the large *shiwahuaco* tree, we drank *ayahuasca*. As we were about to start the ceremony, the sky turned black, and it began to thunder. We could hear the rain close to us. In the jungle when it rains, you can hear the rain approaching from a distance with a roaring sound, until it hits the area where you are and usually comes down in a deluge.

Hearing the rain, everyone ran to the house. Staying where I was, I grabbed my pipe and began to blow the smoke in the direction of the rain. *Maestro* Tuno, Eduardo Calderon, was there watching me. I moved my *báculo*, my staff, to ward off the rain spirits. The *báculo* didn't have as many decorations as it has now, because during the many trips I've done I've received many gifts that now adorn it. The rain continued, but it didn't fall on the tree, which was only about sixty meters away from the house, where it finally was raining. All the people thought it was raining by the tree, so they stayed in the house. At last, the rain left the area.

I went to get the people and said, "Let's start the ceremony." Although everything around us was still wet, my table was completely dry and already had candles and lanterns burning.

"It hasn't rained here!" they said.

"Agustin made the rain go away," said *maestro* Tuno. "It didn't rain here when Agustin blew the smoke to change the direction of the rain."

Although Don Ramon didn't usually drink *ayahuasca* anymore — after a shaman has drunk *ayahuasca* many hundreds of times, maybe thousands, the body can't tolerate it any more — Arimuya asked him to drink a little with us, and he agreed. Before the lights were turned off and the ceremony was about to start, he fell on the ground, completely unconscious. As a result, I was left to run the ceremony on my own. This was the first time I'd had to take the full responsibility. Fortunately I knew how to blow the harmonica, and I had my own *mariris* and *icaros*. By the time the ceremony was over, I had danced, whistled, and sung for five or six hours, while Don Ramon was still asleep.

I remain grateful to Don Ramon because he allowed me to

master the *ayahuasca* when he fell down, and afterwards he graduated me two or three times.

When we returned home, Don Ramon was sad and troubled because he had fallen down due to the *ayahuasca*.

One time when another group had come with Arimuya, Don Eduardo Calderon had come along as well, as he used to travel and work with him at that time.

The night designated for the *ayahuasca* ceremony was beautiful. It had been a good day. We'd heard the birds singing and the jaguars roaring in the middle of the jungle. I offered the *salud*, the offering of thanks and good health which we always do at the beginning of the ceremony before drinking *ayahuasca*. Then I saw that *maestro* Calderon had thrown away the *ayahuasca* in his glass without drinking. So I took the bottle and served him again, saying, "*Maestro*, I want to drink with you, and you have thrown away your *ayahuasca*."

"All right," he said, and drank the cup in front of me.

Afterwards I asked him, "Why did you throw the *ayahuasca* away?" He replied he had seen demons and that I was going to be thrown out of that camp and should be careful.

At the time, I didn't believe him, but it turned out he was right. I was forced out because the cocaine manufacturers eventually moved into the area and started to plant *coca* (the bush used to obtain cocaine hydrochloride), working with the many drug traffickers who passed through. I had to leave as it became very dangerous to be there, and I didn't want to get involved with the *coca* business.

Whenever the groups would come with Arimuya, I'd make thirty pipes, and sell each pipe for a hundred dollars. The people would also buy all my sculptures which helped me tremendously. Today we do the same in my retreat, Yushintaita, where students carve pipes and other items for sale.

After a while Arimuya started inviting me to come along with the groups he was taking to other areas of Peru. He'd pay me to accompany them to Lima, Nazca, Cuzco, the Sacred Valley, and Machu Picchu. On these trips I was responsible for preventing rain and accidents. This was because one time when we were at the airport near the Nazca lines, I told the group we shouldn't fly, and they didn't. Although an airplane didn't crash that day, one did crash another day. I had sensed danger because the stones in my *báculo* (ceremonial staff) were shining red, which signifies danger to me.

On one of the trips while we were at the hotel in Nazca, one of the women in the group became sick with a terrible diarrhea, so acute we had to return to Lima. No medicine was working for her. They hadn't told me anything about the problem until three days had passed and she couldn't get up. Then they called me to tell me she was gravely ill. I went into the hotel's big garden, which had *chirimoya*, *guayaba*, and mango plants. From the *guayaba* I took the fresh leaves, ground them in a blender, and took a glassful of the liquid extract to the woman. We then started for Lima on the bus. From the moment I gave her the extract of ground *guayaba* leaf, she only went to the bathroom once.

By the time we arrived in Lima, this woman had no diarrhea, having been healed by the *guayaba* leaf. When Arimuya saw this happening, he said, "Aguchito can do miracles."

When we arrived in Cuzco, on our way to the Inca Trail, Don Faustino Espinosa, an old Quechua professor from Cuzco University, came to meet me. I wanted to introduce him to Arimuya. Don Faustino is the author of the lyrics of some of my *mariris*, and I had taken some cassettes of my *mariris* to give to him as a gift.

Don Faustino told us we would not be able to travel along the Inca Trail because at that time of the year it rained every day and there was no sun.

Consequently, three *shamans* got together, two from the States and myself, to invoke the kind of weather we wanted for the next day. We started to invoke the spirit of the sun, *Inti*, asking for good weather. *Inti Huasi* is the house of the sun, and the Incas had their temple to the sun in Cuzco.

The next day dawned with incredible sunshine although there

hadn't been any sun for three weeks. Later, at one point on the trail, it began to rain a bit, and Arimuya came over and said, "Aguchito, are we going to have a bad night?"

"No, I'm going to blow it away," I said. I began to blow with my pipe, and the rain stopped immediately. The spirits were taking notice of what I asked. I had to blow away storms as many times as they threatened, but it never rained even once.

That afternoon there was a white fog, like smoke. Arimuya told me, "Aguchito, make this fog disappear, because Machu Picchu is there and we want to see the light reflected on it before nighttime."

"Okay," I said. "But make everybody come over here with their pipes." Everybody had their pipes that I'd sold to them. I told them, "Put tobacco in your pipes. Everybody is going to light the *shimitapon* at the same time, and we are all going to blow three times at the same time so that the work is not only mine but yours, too. Lift your hands, with your pipe in your hands. Worship the spirits, who will give us everything we ask for." Everybody lit their pipes eagerly, and blew with force. Immediately, the fog lifted like a curtain and Machu Picchu appeared.

The next day the weather was warm. We were going to have lunch in Machu Picchu, and as we arrived at the Machu Picchu restaurant, a terrible storm started. The storm had waited for us to reach there. This might have been a coincidence, or it might have been the result of the energies we had called on to help us. There are gods that can see us and hear us. They don't want us to doubt them, and so they give us certain miracles, which help our lives and heal our problems.

Altogether I made twelve trips with Arimuya and his groups. On one of the trips we went to Sillustani, two and a half hours from Puno by car or by bus. After the visit I dreamed strange things and saw that the Aymaras (highland Indians of Peru and Bolivia) didn't like it that we were wandering around that sacred place. I also clearly envisioned what had happened there in ancient times — that they were tall, hardworking people, and that the first inhabitants had arrived in spaceships from other planets. The people of

Cuzco don't like this theory but prefer to believe the Inca creation myth. According to this myth, the Sun sent his own son, Manco Capac, to earth to spread enlightenment and culture, and the Moon sent her daughter, Mama Ocllo, to earth to be his bride. The two of them emerged from Lake Titicaca, near the Islands of the Sun and the Moon. They began a long journey searching for the place where their kingdom would be, which would be found when the golden staff that Manco Capac carried would sink deep into the earth. When they came to the fertile valley of Cuzco, the golden rod sank deep into the soil, and the Incan capital city of Cuzco, meaning "navel of the earth" was founded, and their empire begun.

In 1989, Arimuya invited me to the United States, sending another man to take me there. I took a bottle of very concentrated *ayahuasca* with me, which I prepared especially for the journey. It was my first time to the United States, and for me it was like a journey to the sky because I'd already gone there in my visions. I already knew the United States and Europe through my dreams and visions.

Leaving from Lima, we were in the air when I heard a sound like something exploding above my head in the upper compart-ment. I had the *ayahuasca* in a glass jar wrapped in clothes, placed in several plastic bags, and very well tied up. Many people heard the sound, and I could see the puzzled expressions on their faces. I was waiting for the *ayahuasca* to start dripping, but nothing happened. The *ayahuasca* was fermented, and I told my American friend "It's not dripping, so the plastic bags aren't broken."

When we arrived at a hotel in San Francisco, I removed the *ayahuasca* from my duffel bag. The plastic bag looked like a ball, because the plastic had inflated like a balloon. When I opened it, the glass jar was broken into little pieces. It was a catastrophe!

We decided to pick out all the glass pieces, which we spent several hours doing. All the clothes that had been wrapped around the bottle were saturated with *ayahuasca*, so we wrung them out, trying to save some of it. Getting a plastic jar in the hotel, we poured all the *ayahuasca* into it, together with all the fine glass pieces, since we couldn't filter it. We were concerned that if we drank this *ayahuasca* it could damage our stomachs.

After driving by car to someone's home in Saratoga, we again worked with this liquid. I'd also brought some *ayahuasca* in vines to plant, and so we planted them in this man's garden in Saratoga. We boiled the clothes and rescued the extract from them. Next we used a paper coffee filter to strain the *ayahuasca* and eliminate the glass. Then we cooked it again to make sure it was safe to drink.

Two days later, three of us traveled by car to Sedona, Arizona, on our way to Santa Fe. That night we did an *ayahuasca* ceremony on the banks of a small river in Sedona, when a huge thunderstorm came down and the river started to rise. We were in a tent doing the ceremony, and we had to abandon the site and set up our tent on higher ground. We couldn't see anything because it was so dark, and we had no flashlights. We had to calculate our way up through the rocks. Up there, in the storm with all the lightning, we thought that a bolt could hit us. As a result, we hardly had any visions or sensations during the ceremony, perhaps because of all the turmoil of our surroundings.

At dawn we went to a small hotel that had a bungalow with three beds, a refrigerator, a kitchen, and washing machine, where we stayed for a night to rest.

We continued on through Arizona, arriving towards evening at a section of the desert that was a national park. The other two wanted me to do a ceremony right there but parking was prohibited. Nobody could stay in that place at three hundred feet below sea level, because it was so extremely hot. In ancient times it had been a large ocean that had dried up, leaving only a desert of sand and wind. Because we could not park there, we just went off the road and into the sand about two hundred meters from the road.

That night the moon was full, and according to newspapers and radio announcements, a planetary collision was to occur. We could see very clearly in the desert because the moon was so bright. It was impossible to wear clothes because of the heat, so we took them off, situating ourselves by some dry trees. The wind was blowing the sand along the ground, sighing in the air as it collided against our bodies and against the dry plants. Sitting to start the ceremony, we realized that the sand was going to cover us if we didn't move. We drank the *ayahuasca* but had to constantly move around to avoid being buried by sand. We hardly had any visions because of the distractions around us and the need to remain alert.

At about nine that evening, we heard a loud noise as the planets collided. It sounded as though a bomb had exploded somewhere on the earth, but it had happened in space. Around two in the morning, we left. The car was almost completely covered with sand, and we had to clear it off with our hands. Luckily we were traveling in a four-wheel drive vehicle. We headed towards Santa Fe, where some people were waiting for our arrival. When we got to Santa Fe, we slept a little and then did an *ayahuasca* ceremony outside under the trees. That night the *ayahuasca* ceremony was very good, since *ayahuasca* needs to be taken in silence and tranquility, and in a temperate climate.

The next day they took me to visit Bruce Lamb, the author of two books about the well-known and respected healer Manuel Córdova-Rios. We discussed his books, the jungle, and Manuel Córdova-Rios, whom I'd met when I was a young man. Bruce Lamb, who was by then an old man, invited us for breakfast and gave me a manuscript of an autobiographical book he'd written — which I still have and treasure.

After this we drove to Arimuya's home, in Palo Alto, California, where I met his wife and young son. It was my birthday, and they were waiting for us to celebrate. While I was in California, I held numerous ceremonies and did healings.

From there I traveled to New York and I met up with one of the women who had started to bring her own groups to work with me in the jungle; in New York I did another *ayahuasca* ceremony.

Afterwards I traveled to Europe, then back to Pucallpa.

There I learned that a third administrator of the lumber company cutting timber around my encampment had died. Since the time I'd played my drums and it rained for a whole month, many things had happened. The huge forest tractors which lifted the wood had ceased working because they had sunk deeply into the mud of the jungle, and three people had now died.

Chapter 19
Shamanic Graduation

In between my travels around Peru with Arimuya's groups, I'd go back to Pucallpa. There I continued working on my sculptures with increased creativity because the places we'd visited were sacred places of power and gave me a lot of energy.

I also had earned money by accompanying the groups, and I was able to buy art supplies and to pay my wife's debts from buying on credit from the stores.

After the last trip, I went to visit Don Ramon. He greeted me, "Good morning Aguchito! How's it going? I heard that you left for Lima, because I went to visit you and you weren't home. Soronjita told me you'd left with the group to Cuzco and Puno and all around."

Don Ramon told me there was going to be an *ayahuasca* ceremony on Friday. There were some Austrian people visiting me at my home, and I invited them to the ceremony. At that time there were a lot of tourists in Pucallpa, but not now, due to terrorism. The Austrians were happy to drink *ayahuasca* with Don Ramon, and they had good visions, all night long.

During the ceremony, Don Ramon said, "Come on Aguchito, sing now."

I was surprised because he had never asked me to sing before during one of his ceremonies.

"Yes, you must be a great master already!" he said, a little sarcastically.

I already knew many *mariris* of my own, which were totally different from the ones Don Ramon sang, and said, "Don Ramon, you gave me strength, you graduated me, and I want to do my best to sing for you."

I began to sing, and Don Ramon said, "How beautiful!" He'd never heard a student sing. No one was allowed to sing without his authorization. The student must always wait for the teacher to provide the opportunity. I continued singing and playing my *arco* (stringed bow-shaped instrument).

"Very good," he said, "You made me fly."

"All right, Don Ramon, if you want, I can keep on singing."

He agreed, so I began to blow my harmonica, and shake my *maracas*, and he was almost dancing. Don Ramon was surprised at how much I had learned, and that I wasn't copying what he did.

The next night when I was asleep at home, Don Ramon and his wife, Doña Francisca, appeared to me in a dream. Very clearly, Don Ramon said to me, "Aguchito, I want to graduate you, I want you to have *alto muraya*." Then his wife said, "Yes Don Aguchito, you are *alto muraya*. What Don Ramon says is true. It's your graduation."

"Thank you, Doña Francisca, thank you, Don Ramon," I told them, happily. Then I woke up, and said to Soronjita, "Don Ramon just graduated me, I'm *alto muraya*."

"It must be true! Surely Don Ramon was thinking of you," she said.

At dawn I went directly over to see Don Ramon, arriving there at about seven. That morning Don Ramon was cultivating his orchard and he hadn't gone to the jungle yet. Sometimes he wasn't easy to find, because he'd go to the jungle to collect medicinal plants for his patients.

I said, "Good morning, Don Ramoncito."

"Good morning, Aguchito. What brings you here today?"

"Don Ramon, did you dream anything last night?" I asked.

"Why? I think I dreamed something about you," he answered.

Then Doña Francisca came over and said, "Last night I dreamed about Don Agustin."

"What did you dream, Doña Francisca?" I asked.

"I don't remember well," she said.

"Well, last night I saw you both in a dream, and you were graduating me."

"Ha, ha, ha!" Don Ramon laughed. "Oh, really! How did it go?"

"You were very serious, and Doña Francisca was standing next to you. You called me and said that from now on I was *alto muraya*."

Don Ramon, laughing like a *brujo*, said, "Then it must be true. So you're graduated. Probably my spirit graduated you! You're going to be better than me because I didn't have a graduation. Imagine that, Francisca, Don Aguchito is *alto muraya*!"

I told Don Ramon I was grateful to him and gave him some tobacco and perfume that I'd brought. The old man had many perfumes that I'd given to him as gifts, and he prepared them with his *icaros* to bless his clients. He'd always bless me with his perfumes, so I'd have luck in love with women and with business. "This is for having women Aguchito, you'll have lots of them. Ha, ha, ha!" he'd say, laughing.

Then we picked bags of oranges, grapefruits, and guavas from his orchard for me to take to my family.

Before I left, he said, "Don't forget that we'll have another ceremony on Tuesday. Come and maybe I'll graduate you to *altomando muraya*!"

"Don Ramon, I don't believe that the next graduation will be so soon, many years will have to pass," I answered.

"That's right," he said. "You have to continue dieting."

"I've been dieting so much, Don Ramon, that I don't want to go on diets anymore. I've dieted from 1971 to 1975, and I think it's enough."

"No, if you are going to be *altomando muraya*, you have to diet more, and if you're going to be *banco*, you'll have to diet for one year."

"Oh, I'll have to give up having sex, and I cannot do that. I can't now, my life has changed," I answered.

"It depends on you, Aguchito," he told me. Then I thanked him and left.

Because I needed more *renaco* roots, I went with a young man, seventeen years old, to the jungle swamps where the *renaco* trees grew. There were many boas, eels, and other snakes there, as well as a lot of *piripiral*, an herb that grows in the water.

I'd built a bridge there, about twenty meters (sixty feet) long, so I could cross to the other side. I was crossing over, with the young man a little behind me, when I heard him screaming. I turned to look and saw him enveloped by a boa as wide as a dog. It had wrapped him so tightly he could barely shout; he was so deprived of air and strength. I shouted and ran towards him carrying my pistol. But then I thought that a bullet could go into the young man's body, so I grabbed my knife instead and began attacking the boa. I stabbed and stabbed until the boa began to unwind from the young man. It even tried to pull me, despite my stabbing.

When it had uncoiled, the head was biting into the boy's pants. I grabbed its head, which was as big as two hands, and cut its throat. Destroying the teeth with my knife, I managed to pull its head away from the young man's pants.

The boy was standing silent, absolutely terrorized, knowing that he'd almost been killed by the boa. I had to slap him twice to snap him out of his shock. I had the head of the boa in my hand, so it wouldn't escape, and the skull bones were all fractured.

I told him to cut down a vine with his machete, and we wrapped it around the boa's head and started to pull the boa along. The boa was long, and the tail was caught inside the mud wrapped around some root because it was trying to keep it's power to hold on. We pulled harder and harder, while the boa was gradually dying. Then the tail broke free, and we finally pulled it out.

No longer looking for roots, we both pulled the boa, which weighed more than 150 kilos. Finally we were able to get it to my workshop. There we skinned it. Since we had no nails we had to use little sticks to keep the skin spread open. Extracting more than eight bottles of boa fat, we then threw the meat away, far off. We don't eat the meat of a boa. There were duck bones and legs in it's bowels, which hadn't been digested, but no human parts. Apparently, it had been eating birds, but this time wanted to eat a human. Today I still have the skin of this thirty-feet-long boa at my home in Pucallpa.

I'd been down in that same place some days before without my rifle. That day this same boa had appeared when some kids had gone to pick guavas from the trees, called *shimbillos*. The boa came over, moving the grass in the water, while the children were in a tree, wanting to eat them. I shouted, and the boa looked at me with huge eyes, then took off. The kids came down the tree and went to get a rifle to kill it, but when they returned with the rifle, the boa had disappeared.

In that same place an eel once almost electrified me, so I shot it. It was a giant eel about six feet long and about ten inches in diameter. Such swampy places, where *renaco* trees grow, are called *renacales*, and are full of all kinds of dangerous animals.

When I returned to Pucallpa, I went to see a journalist, who wrote about the boa. He said, "The sculptor, Agustin Rivas, killed a giant boa that was trapping a youngster in Yarinacocha. If the sculptor had not been present, the giant boa would have eaten this young man." After that people began to visit me, to see the huge skin.

I also sold the boa lard in liter bottles at fifty *soles* each. Boa fat is very expensive because it's applied to damaged bones which have been dislocated due to an accident. We apply the fat and then we wrap the bone up with an elastic gauze. After five or ten minutes, the bone begins to move back to it's original place, but this treatment is terribly painful.

I experienced this cure once when I had an accident on my Lambretta motorcycle, and dislocated my ankle. When I got home, I didn't feel much pain, but in the night my ankle started hurting a lot, and it was swollen. A *sobadora* (bone doctor), Doña Soledad Macedo, came over to massage the ankle, but this made it hurt even more, and the bone didn't go back into place. Then when she came back another night, she brought boa fat and applied it to my ankle and wrapped it in an elastic gauze. I lay on the bed for an hour, and the pain was so unbearable I untied the bandage, and the bone didn't go back in place. The next day Doña Soledad asked me if the bone had gone back in place, and I told her I had removed the bandage because I couldn't stand the pain.

She told me I shouldn't have taken the bandage off and applied the boa fat again, wrapping it up tightly with the bandage. In half an hour or so, the unbearable pain came back, but I had to endure it. Excruciating pain occurs when the bone begins to move back into the right place. Soon I heard, "Crack!" as the bone went back into place, and then the pain stopped.

In 1991, I moved back to Tamshiyacu. In Pucallpa terrorism had begun, and around my encampment Empire of Youth, *coca* had been planted. It had become a red zone, and we could no longer take tourists there.

At the time living conditions were terrible in Pucallpa, since the terrorists charged a fee to everyone, including store owners, workers, builders, and winery owners, for their right to be free. They also came to the small store Soronjita ran to charge us a fee, but my wife told them we weren't selling anything.

The terrorists wandered around Pucallpa freely, but if the police saw them they were sent to jail. Many people died, bombs exploded in the city, and policemen were killed on the highway. There weren't any parties, and musicians who made a living from their music no longer had work. We couldn't celebrate birthdays, weddings, or any other festivity.

Consequently I returned to Tamshiyacu with a woman from Arimuya's groups, who had started bringing her own groups to work with me at Empire of Youth. I told her, "You're not coming to Pucallpa anymore, you're coming to Iquitos." She wanted to be my partner and start a shamanic work center in Tamshiyacu, so we began on the land where I had been born, called Nuevo Tarapoto. One of the local *brujos* accompanied us, but I didn't like his energy and didn't ask him to work with us anymore.

This woman gave a thousand dollars to Eladio, who was the son-in-law of my uncle and aunt, to build a house. This young man was learning shamanism with me, and he recorded all my songs and began to learn them quickly. He believed that by singing my songs he could become an *ayahuasquero* shaman and a healer. Eladio used the thousand dollars to build a house about ten meters high. When the woman came back to Tamshiyacu again, she found the house built, but it wasn't worth the money she'd given him. However, Eladio said that he'd spent the money on the house, and so there was nothing she could do about it.

With a small group of about eight people this woman had brought with her, we had an *ayahuasca* ceremony in the house with Eladio. But we soon found out there was not enough privacy in the area. There was too much noise so close to the town, and people watched us and interrupted our ceremony. As a result, I decided to look for a more remote place.

Then my uncle Eugenio came and told me, "Let's go to a *colpa* (a place where many animals go to drink water and eat salty clay), where you'll see a beautiful place." He brought me to see this place — where I now have my encampment, Yushintaita — and I saw a beautiful river, with wonderfully clear water. Inspecting the area, I saw how the river wound its way through it, and how beautiful and serene the environment was. So I decided I would establish an encampment there.

I started immediately looking for workers to build the big house that is now here in Yushintaita, which we use as a dormitory when groups come. At first it didn't have wooden boards, it had *ponas*, strips made from the bark of the palm tree, and it was open sided, with only a big mosquito net in the middle, about seven or eight meters by seven meters wide. When the first groups came, we had the ceremonies inside this mosquito net. A kitchen was built next and then gradually, the other small houses that are here, including the one in which I now live. Eventually, a temple was built at a distance from the sleeping area, where we continue to hold the ceremonies. Each year we have improved all the buildings and facilities.

Over the years there have been many remarkable healings that have taken place through the *ayahuasca* ceremonies. For example, one concerned a man whose madness was healed. He came here to the jungle, over a period of about four years, maybe once sometimes twice a year, with the groups that would come. He would tremble all the time, and he couldn't connect his thoughts with the rhythm of the music. Finally he was able to focus on the problem that had caused his trauma. During his visions, he saw that because he cried and shit a lot his father had wanted to kill him when he was a baby, by hanging him by the legs and beating him, and that his mother had saved him from being killed. He saw his father hanging him by the feet to hit him, and that it was then that his brain had been damaged. Because of this he'd lost his sanity and been crazy his whole life.

Later, I encountered the man again in a different setting when I had traveled to New Jersey to do a ceremony for a group. About two in the morning, close to the end of the ceremony, I was playing music with my harmonica and my rattle. After a while I heard somebody in the corner of the room, accompanying me with the rattle, and I could hear that the rhythm was perfectly synchronized with mine. Many people try and play the rattle with me, but they can't follow my music exactly. Then I speeded up my playing, to show the person who was playing the rattle, that they had to follow my rhythm exactly, without interrupting the rhythm for the visions. The person speeded up with me, and the rhythm was perfect. I wondered who it was, and I went over to the corner and saw that it was this man who'd been crazy previously, unable to follow any rhythm.

The first time he had come to the jungle, he couldn't even beat the drum. I gave him the drum to play, and he couldn't. I blew the *antara* (panpipes - musical instrument made of bamboo tubes), and he couldn't follow the rhythm, neither using the drum or the rattle. I thought, "This man has a problem, something is going on with his brain that makes him unable to coordinate his movements." I wanted to discover what his problem was, like a psychiatrist does with his patients.

However, that night in New Jersey he was playing perfectly, and I told him so. I was happy to see he'd recovered.

The next day, as we always do after the ceremonies, we had a meeting so everybody could recount their visions. This man said, "This is my last ceremony. I feel I'm totally healed, and I'm not going to have any more *ayahuasca*. Don Agustin heard my rattle when I was playing with him, and it means that the communication system between my arms and my brain is working well. I'm happy that my treatment is finished."

Another interesting healing that occurred concerned a man who had also come to the jungle, a psychiatrist who taught at a University in New Jersey and had a home office where he treated patients. When we had *ayahuasca* ceremonies at his home, his patients would take part and felt good afterwards.

This psychiatrist practiced a therapy which involved putting his patients in a closed room and playing very loud music. He'd remain in there with them, and it appeared that in the process of the patients releasing their traumas, the illnesses would go into this psychiatrist's body. As a result, he began to have serious problems with his wife.

I told him that that he shouldn't be inside that room with his patients, saying, "They have transmitted terrible things to you, and that's why your brain isn't working well. You're having problems with your wife. You're not in good mental condition, you're very sick."

Subsequently, he came to the jungle twice to heal his problem. In his visions the *ayahuasca* told him not to continue his psychiatric work. He was shown images of his own insides and crazy nerves, and he began to see strange pictures in his visions of demonic, colorful things. As a result, he left the university, quit being a psychiatrist, and started devoting himself to painting what he had seen inside himself.

On my next visit to New York, I went to see him at his house. He'd done some paintings expressing his spiritual problems, his madness, and his intentions. He was painting with intense colors that reflected the feeling of madness. Later, he began to sell his paintings at a very good price and was earning more money than he had at the university.

On another of my trips I was in Brooklyn, and this psychiatrist called to say he wanted me to come see him because he didn't go out of his home anymore and just stayed there painting. When I went over to his place, he had more than twenty beautiful paintings finished. The first ones had very intense colors in them, and then, progressively with each new painting, the colors became softer and clearer. I thought immediately that he was healing. During his madness his wife had divorced him, but after he was cured by *ayahuasca*, they remarried. Now, he is a famous painter who makes $5,000 a painting. Although he doesn't usually leave his house, he is not crazy.

Ayahuasca can produce miraculous cures, but this sometimes takes time. When we work constantly with the same person over the years, we eventually find their problem. While many people cannot heal with one ceremony, but need to experience several, others heal during the very first *ayahuasca* ceremony. They change their thinking, their imaginations expand, they are filled with creativity, and sometimes they change their jobs, following the advice of mother *ayahuasca*.

Ayahuasca is the death vine, the plant through which we can experience death, or in some cases a physical disappearance, but then return. A transmutation can take place, whereby our body and soul can travel through space, and heal someone, visit distant places, or go home to where our families or loved ones are. Many hours can go by without any awareness that time has passed. During four or five hours the shaman works with the people, healing them through his dancing, music, *mariris*, *icaros*, and blowing of tobacco. If there are sick people, the shaman some-times needs to suck out the illness.

At one *ayahuasca* ceremony in New York, there was a young man who was sitting in a corner where there was a climbing plant that had heart-shaped leaves. The room wasn't totally dark, but only dim. During the ceremony, when I looked, the man wasn't there in his chair. "Where's your friend?" I asked the other partic-ipants.

"He's here," they said.

"How strange that this man is not in his place. He needs to be in the room with us," I replied. I was concerned because I couldn't see him anywhere. I then looked for him all over the small house. He couldn't have gone out, I realized, because my ceremonial table was blocking the door.

Then suddenly I saw him drop down into the plants like a light and sit down on his chair.

"Where have you been?" I asked.

"I've been traveling," he said.

"How strange! You haven't been in your seat, and now I see you come down from the sky, from the plants!" I answered. The plants had somehow absorbed him mysteriously. This happened twice with this same man.

It was an extraordinary event for the people there, and they started to invite more people to other ceremonies, which they arranged in a bigger room in New York. This young man came again, inviting his entire family to see the magical things that happened during the *ayahuasca* ceremony. The ceremonies became more beautiful each time, and more and more people started attending, until we had about sixty people at a ceremony.

At another ceremony in New York, two doctors brought an AIDS patient to take part. We gave him a separate cup to drink from and separated him a little from the other participants because his state was critical. The doctors wanted to see if I could help him. I wasn't afraid of AIDS, and had sucked the illness from many AIDS patients — from their foreheads — and I've never gotten this illness. I worked a lot with this patient, blowing tobacco, and pulling the illness from a distance. When the illness gets to me, it generally dies.

The next morning at breakfast, this AIDS patient's whole color had changed. When he'd first arrived, he was a somber deadly color of yellow; now he looked pink. Moreover, his hemoglobin had been very low when he first came, about eight or nine, so he was very anemic. Later, when the doctors took him to have a blood analysis two days after the ceremony, his hemoglobin was twelve. Although he seemed improved, I never heard from him again and don't know if he has survived.

Once I was doing a ceremony in the meeting room of a hotel in Germany. A filmmaker whose camera had infrared capabilities, filmed the ceremony, capturing the spirit of a sick person on film. They'd brought a sick German man for me to operate on, and many people had come to see this.

After everybody had drunk *ayahuasca*, including the filmmaker, I began to operate on this man, who was about sixty years old. When he came into the room, he could barely walk and was leaning forward using two walking sticks. As I performed the surgery, the camera filmed everything that occurred. Light rays, red lights, black lights, and blue lights, were captured on film. When the healing was over, I brought the man into the center of the room and began to massage the areas of the surgery. The ceremony went on with many participants happy to experience a plant that allows a person to see their life situation. Finally, everyone went off to sleep.

In the morning we all went to breakfast. It was a four-star hotel, luxurious, with flowers all around and a breakfast buffet decorated with many different cheeses, fruits, and breads. We were starting to eat when I saw this man come down the stairs without his walking sticks. People started applauding as he came in to have breakfast.

My belief is that a shaman is a humble and simple person, who works without the idea of monetary gain, and doesn't charge for healing and treatments. Here at my encampment, I charge for lodging and food but not for healing or for operations. You cannot buy or sell the life of a patient; and you cannot tell a patient how much their life or their healing is worth, and if they don't have money, refuse to do it. A shaman cannot do this because his healing is spiritual, and because of his faith, healing occurs. A shaman cannot charge for anybody's life, because love and faith in spirit don't function in this way.

Chapter 20
The Mystery of Boa Fat

I always came back from working in the United States with money to keep improving my encampment. I needed to keep building more houses, because groups were coming constantly. Over the year the work had increased here dramatically.

Once I invited Don Ramon because many people coming with the groups were curious to meet him. I went to get him in Pucallpa, and from there we flew to Iquitos, staying in a hotel, to await the group's arrival. While we were there, I went to the Belen market and bought some black boa fat or boa butter. There are two kinds of boas, yellow and black. The black is more aggressive, and has a much finer fat. When I came back from the market, I told him I'd bought black boa butter. But, after opening the bag, I found that one of the bottles was leaking. All of the wrappings were soaked in the boa fat, and to avoid wasting it, I began to rub it all over my body.

Marlena, the woman I now live with, was with me, and she said, "Let's go and visit my aunt. She's in Iquitos." We did this, and while drinking tea at her aunt's house, I started feeling that something was pushing me down towards the floor, I felt feverish, and I could hardly stand. I didn't know what was wrong with me, and the thought that it could be the boa fat didn't even enter my mind.

By the time we returned to the hotel, I had a very high fever, and my body was trembling. Don Ramon was there waiting because he was coming to Yushintaita with me.

Before we'd gone out, I'd given a young man who worked in

the hotel the papers saturated with the boa fat to throw away. He'd gotten some of the fat on his hands, then gone home and held a baby. Now the baby also had a fever and contortions, and nobody knew why. The next day he came and told me that they had taken the baby to the doctor, who said that the boa fat had caused the problem.

Boa fat is very mysterious and marvelous. It's not a poison, but it has powerful energy, and that's why it can make bones go back into place when they are dislocated. It's also good for the nerves. Many people don't like the fishy smell it has.

It was the first time that I had such a reaction to boa fat. The skin on my legs, arms, and stomach began to peel, and it was as if I had a new skin, so I assumed it must be doing something beneficial to my body. Don Ramon came to my bedroom to blow tobacco on me, but it had no effect, and the fever continued for three days.

When the group arrived, we all went off to Tamshiyacu by boat. Arriving at my jungle encampment Yushintaita, everybody treated Don Ramon with a lot of consideration and gave him many gifts.

When we were in Iquitos, Don Ramon had told me, "Aguchito, go and buy three bottles of wine and two of rum."

"What are you going to do with that?" I asked.

"It's to make medicine."

At Yushintaita, we accommodated Don Ramon in a little house, together with a young man, Marcos, also from Pucallpa, who had a drug addiction problem, and whom I'd brought along to heal. He came by boat, and Don Ramon came with me by plane.

We had a meeting where I introduced Don Ramon officially, explaining that he was my teacher and that I'd spent many years taking *ayahuasca* with him. Everybody was happy to meet him. Before the first ceremony Don Ramon told me he was going to graduate me to *altomando muraya*. We went to the temple, where Don Ramon did the first part of the ceremony. He began to sing. I was listening and a bit dizzy with the *ayahuasca*, but not really having visions like I often did. I've now had so much experience with *ayahuasca* that it has to be a very strong brew for me to have visions.

About halfway through the ceremony, Don Ramon told me that it was my turn. So I began to sing and dance for about an hour. In the meantime, Don Ramon was preparing his *shimitapon* (his pipe) with tobacco, singing in a low voice, and putting prayers into the tobacco that I was going to smoke. It was a very large pipe that he'd made when he was doing a special diet, and he'd only smoked that pipe with me and with nobody else.

"Rest a bit," he said, "the graduation ceremony is going to start. First, you're going to smoke this pipe."

When I started to smoke the pipe, he told me to swallow the smoke. Swallowing the smoke, together with the effects of the *ayahuasca*, made the dizziness and intoxication terrible! I thought that Don Ramon was either trying to knock me out to avoid graduating me, or testing me to see if I had the endurance to be graduated. People knew I was graduating so everybody was paying attention, and, at the same time, they were seeing their own visions.

My legs were trembling, my nerves were weakening, my ears were roaring, the *urcututus* (owls) were singing, and I knew I was going to either fall, or endure. I knew I had to endure this test in order to graduate, and I wanted to take advantage of the opportunity that Don Ramon had given me.

Finally Don Ramon said, "Come and stand in front of the *mesa* (ceremonial table) and keep on smoking the pipe." I had to open my legs up wide to avoid falling. I wanted to vomit, but I wasn't supposed to vomit, so I didn't. Then Don Ramon said, "It's time for the graduation of *maestro* Agustin Rivas. Everyone get up and make a circle." By that time I'd finished smoking the *shimitapon*, which had taken me more than a half hour. He had another *shimitapon*, and he brought it into the circle with him.

Then with his hand on my head, he started to sing and blow smoke on me, saying that I was now a *maestro* who could work at the level of all the great *maestros*. He invoked the spirits of all the elements to come to me, so that I could be a great master of medicine, not only with *ayahuasca* but also with tobacco and other plants. Next he touched my head again, blowing tobacco smoke and perfume onto me, and sang a lovely *mariri*. He said, "Lift your head and look at the sky, look at the spirits that are coming to your graduation. All of them are looking at you, the *Chullachaqui* is coming from the jungle, and the *Yacurunas* are coming from the waters to honor you and to give you all the energy you need, so that you can be, from now on, *altomando muraya*. I graduate you and wish you good luck!"

After this I felt a powerful new energy come into me, and felt my own energy changed. Don Ramon was a very good and powerful man when he appreciated somebody. I continued singing in the ceremony, now with the completely different energy of *altomando muraya*. Everybody could feel my stronger energy. I sang and sang, and I felt different, that I was a *maestro*, that God had blessed me, and that the spirits were protecting me.

The next morning at breakfast, everybody told Don Ramon what a blessing it was to know him, and thanked him for being with us. After breakfast, we got together for our meeting to talk about the ceremony, and some participants asked Don Ramon to explain about it.

"Well, it was very nice, didn't you like it?" he said.

"Yes, Don Ramon, we liked it," they answered.

"So if you liked it, that's very good. It was Aguchito's graduation ceremony, and it was very good. He deserves it and he's a good friend. But among you there are many sick people. You're seriously sick." He focused this last comment to four men who were sitting in the front.

"Tell us Don Ramon, what do we have," they asked.

"No, I'm not going to tell you today, I'll tell you tomorrow in a private consultation," he replied.

I knew that surely he wanted some money. Then he said, "I only want you to remember this old man with something, because I'm also poor."

Later, people began to gather about five or six hundred dollars for Don Ramon, which he received in the afternoon and he was happy.

In the evening he left for his little house with Marcos, the young man who had come from Pucallpa for a healing, and Manuel, a young man from Tamshiyacu. Manuel didn't drink but Marcos did, and so he and Don Ramon drank the three bottles of wine and the two bottles of rum while the rest of us were sleeping.

In the morning we had a meeting, and waited for Don Ramon to explain what illnesses the men had. Meanwhile Don Ramon was lying on the floor of his hut intoxicated, having drunk all the alcohol the night before. Manuel came to tell us that Don Ramon wasn't feeling well because he'd drunk *ayahuasca* in the night.

"*Ayahuasca?*" I said, "How can he have *ayahuasca* alone if he never wants to even drink in groups. It's worse by himself." I went over and saw all the empty bottles of alcohol. "How incredible!"

All day Don Ramon was drunk, speaking nonsense such as, "I'm a poor old man and nobody cares, nobody pays attention to me. I have to die like this, abandoned by everybody. Nobody loves me." There was a translator, and so everyone knew what he was saying. The Americans were surprised at what was happening.

One came over to me and asked, "Did Don Ramon drink *ayahuasca* last night?"

"No, he drank wine and rum!" I couldn't lie to them, because he hadn't drunk *ayahuasca*.

That night we were having another ceremony. The sun set, and we were ready to go to the temple when Don Ramon announced, "I'm not going, I'm annoyed!" This was unfounded since no one had upset him. So, we went to the temple, and Don Ramon didn't show up. Instead he was still drunk and dizzy.

I started the ceremony, my second one since graduating to *altomando muraya*. I felt strong and different, and that the ceremony would be better than the others. The *ayahuasca* was very strong, and at one point everybody was defecating and vomiting. One man went outside and sat on a tree, took off his pants, and shouted. His shouting resonated in the jungle, and he shouted with his heart and soul. The staff and cooks who were in the sleeping area three hundred meters away from the temple could hear him. The next day the man didn't remember that he had been shouting.

The day after the ceremony we had our usual meeting. Don Ramon was around, but he was ashamed so he didn't want to attend the meeting. I knew he was packing to leave, and that he'd asked Manuel to accompany him. They left while we were having the meeting.

Then the man who'd been shouting the night before told us about his vision. He said that in his vision he was shitting music, and the excrement looked like musical notes. Later when we saw his excrement it was incredibly long, like a snake.

"What an experience!" I said, "Was it nice?"

"Yes, singing with the ass is really nice," he answered.

In those times when the groups came to the encampment, I'd often bring fresh cow excrement there. Laying down a big piece of plastic, I'd empty three or four bags of this excrement, which my workers had carried from a field where cattle grazed, and tell the group, "This is a therapy to cleanse your body, and afterwards you're going to have a lot of luck in everything, in your work, in love, and in your health."

One of the women, who'd helped me by giving me $1,000 to buy more land and to build the temple — a very nice, affectionate and generous woman — asked me, "Agustin is this a joke or is it real?"

"It's real." I answered. "You know that in India they don't eat cows, but they use their excrement, and they also eat mushrooms that grow in the excrement. They worship the cows like goddesses. Honoring this, everybody who uses this excrement will cleanse their body. It will penetrate to the heart and to the chakras. This excrement doesn't come from regular cows, it comes from *cebu* cows that have a hump on their backs."

"Oh! very good. Then I'm going to participate with pleasure," she said.

After she had laid down, I had to initiate the work by scooping up excrement with both hands and putting it on her sexual parts and breasts, to cover them so people wouldn't look at them. Then everybody else began to throw excrement on their bodies. I told them they could put it in their mouths too, and many did it, because they believed in this work. Once they were thoroughly covered, they looked like demons. Using the cow excrement also seemed to induce some hallucination.

Next, I told them that we should go into the sun for half an hour until the cow excrement dried. We made a circle, and I started to sing a children's song, which ended with the line, "sit down!", then everyone sat down. There were many small leaves on the ground, and when they'd stand up, after sitting down, there were hundreds of little leaves stuck to their buttocks, which made them laugh. Then everybody began to take pictures with their cameras.

After everybody was dry, their skin was getting warm, and they could feel the skin shrinking and being rejuvenated, we went down to the water to bathe. I took a hard little brush used for the laundry, and began to brush their backs. It was incredible what substances were coming out of their bodies, like green and blue phlegm. Their skin became clean and renewed.

At lunch time, we could still smell shit, "Who hasn't bathed well? Let's check them." Inside some people's ears, in the ear bridge, there was some cow excrement left. "It's stinking, go wash your ears."

In past times in Tamshiyacu when there wasn't a lot of soap, the laundry women used cow excrement to clean clothes. Dissolving it in a bowl they'd place the white shirts in the liquid, and afterwards they were whiter, with all the dirt cleaned off. I remember that my aunt Celedonia used cow excrement to wash with, and the clothes were really white and didn't smell. There isn't a detergent as good as cow excrement to wash clothes.

Many groups continued to come to my encampment for ceremonies and healing, and this helped to buy boats, motors, build better houses, and improve the encampment and services.

With all the payments and guarantees that we make to the Ministry of Tourism, and all the legalities with taxes, there's a lot involved with running this encampment. Although my organization has become very involved, the results continue to be very good.

In addition, I've had very positive results doing ceremonies in Europe, which is where I generally travel for a month or two at a time each year, into different areas of Austria, Germany, Italy and England. There people have loved me a lot, and I enjoyed working with them. My view has always been that every sick person can heal. I've performed many shamanic surgeries, operating on people with cancer and other diseases, through the energy of God and the spirits. People have found my work to be very effective.

In 1991, when I came to my present encampment, I thought that my wife was going to come too, but she preferred to stay in the city. Consequently, I began to have romances with many women, until I found Marlena, a woman from Tamshiyacu whom I met when I returned here. I've stayed with her for eight years, and she helps me with everything, and is an inspiration.

I believe that in all parts of the world where there are shamans the women want to be with them. Although in the past I was a womanizer, at this period in my life, my life has been transformed, and I'm not that old shaman anymore. Today I have a new way of thinking, because love is a very delicate thing. I now see that when a woman falls in love there are emotional and mental problems, so it's better not to be with one unless you are willing to stay with her. If a woman tells me she wants to be with me, I may consider being with her, but I'm not looking for women anymore. I don't have any new women in my life, and only occasionally do I get together with women I've been with in the past.

Many times the participants in ceremonies have seen my guardians, and I've seen them too. They're Indians, well-armed with bows, arrows, and darts, and wearing feathered crowns, with eyes on the backs of their heads, and on both sides. These guardians take care of me, and when I get threatened or hurt in any way, my guardians make whomever or whatever go away, or punish them with illness or death.

Although I don't have intentions of harming anybody, my guardians are cruel, vengeful, and very protective. They know all my intentions are to help people and society find health, love, and tranquility.

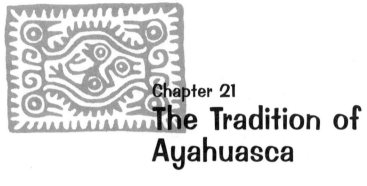

Chapter 21
The Tradition of Ayahuasca

Ayahuasca is a plant that has been used for healing in the Amazon for thousands of years. Before there were hospitals, clinics, and doctors in the area, *ayahuasca* was used to cure people. Even with all the hospitals today, people still come in search of shamans to cure them with the help of *ayahuasca* and other plant medicines.

Ayahuasca is sublime, divine, special. It teaches respect for life and for others. During visions, one can see one's life purpose. Using *ayahuasca* is a shamanic tradition that comes from my ancestors, and has been passed down from generation to generation. I continue making and using it so it will not disappear from our culture.

Ayahuasca is a visionary plant that allows one to see and hear the spirits. For many years, before I used *ayahuasca*, I sensed that the universe was full of spirits. I could sometimes hear their voices in the air, but I could not see them as I do now. The spirits are energies, like radio waves, and you must turn on your radio in order to hear them. Even when *ayahuasca* doesn't produce visions immediately, it is still working on the body, and visions can appear in your dreams, even a month later. It's like a vitamin that keeps working within you.

Ayahuasca is a great shaman and a professor; it will teach anyone who uses it. People can drink *ayahuasca* to gain knowledge about their vocations or professions. A German psychology professor who took *ayahuasca* with me later told his students he had learned much about psychology from the *ayahuasca* that he had never learned at the university.

Ayahuasca has been my university. I have taken it over 1500 times, and it has made me more intelligent and energetic. Drinking *ayahuasca* is like going to school to learn about medicine. It is a teacher who gives prescriptions to shamans.

Ayahuasca is a visionary vine, but it must always be prepared with its counterpart, *chacruna*. The DMT in *chacruna* and the harmine and harmaline in the *ayahuasca* vine work together to induce visions. Sometimes, we add small amounts of *toé* (*datura*) and tobacco to help create specific visions related to the studies that one undertakes to become a shaman.

Ayahuasca heals primarily by faith, but it also allows us to see the mysterious inner workings of our bodies. In our visions, we can witness what is going on inside us, and in the process, cleanse our bodies.

Sometimes while using *ayahuasca*, the shaman can see into the skeleton, the brain, the organs, or the intestines of a person. The shaman is generally not a diviner, so it is usually better to tell him about a pain or illness, so he knows what to cure. However, sometimes the shaman may see something white in the bones and know there is something wrong. If the shaman sees that there is a problem in a part of the body, you can be sure that this is the case since *ayahuasca* won't lie. Usually when the shaman sees a problem, he can clean it out. That's the magic of *ayahuasca*.

Of course, if the shaman sees that the illness is caused by microbes or requires surgery, then he should refer you to doctors so they can work on it. However, today most illnesses are caused by spiritual problems, by stress or fear, or by exposure to pollution and electromagnetic fields. Although people in cities often eat well, they have more health problems than people here in the jungle. Cancer, heart attacks, and ulcers are not caused by microbes or infections, but by overloading the nerves.

Our nervous systems are very sensitive electrical circuits. Everything we take in through our senses — vision, hearing, touch, taste, and smell — travels through our nerves and then ends up getting stored in our neurons. When we overload our nerves, it is like sending a 220-volt current through a 110-volt system; sooner or later it will blow a fuse or start a fire. When we talk and talk senselessly, or listen to the radio all day long, or watch television too much, our neurons get overloaded. When we live in constant drama all the time, our neurons get overloaded. Bad news, bad smells, extremely loud noises all damage our neurons, and this can make us sick or crazy. When our neurons get overloaded, they collapse and stop working. That is why we need to take time to meditate and rest our senses every day.

Sometimes when traumas are very serious — for example, when a child is mistreated by parents, when a young girl is violated during adolescence, or when a person suffers a serious accident — very bad impressions are left on the neurons that can affect many parts of the mind and body.

Everything we have seen, heard, read, or even thought is stored in our brain, and in our neurons. Everything that our senses have received has impressed itself upon the neurons. Even those things that one no longer remembers are stored in the neurons. All these impressions may sleep within our subconscious until something activates them. Then they can come back into our thoughts and make us sick or crazy.

Ayahuasca has the ability to cure and to give new life to the body. When we take *ayahuasca*, it repairs our overloaded neurons. Other drugs contain chemical substances that invade and destroy the neurons, but *ayahuasca* protects and heals them. When *ayahuasca* begins to repair the neurons, it awakens the impressions which have been engraved on them. The neurons return these impressions in the form of visions, because the neurons of the body are connected to the iris of the eye. For example, usually when we see demons in visions, it is the *ayahuasca* showing us manifestations of the traumas, bad thoughts, and poisons that have been stored in our nerves. The *ayahuasca* helps us release the toxins and excess energies stored in our bodies, and we see those energies as demons because that is how we have learned to imagine our negative thoughts.

Society has taught us to imagine our instincts, particularly our antisocial instincts, as demons. Most people think that demons are dark, ugly beings with big teeth, long nails and horns, because that is the way they have been depicted by religions in order to scare people. In reality, most demons are nothing more than negative instincts or energies that have been given the form of demons in our imagination. In the same way, good energies often manifest in the form of angels, because we have been taught to associate angels with good energies.

Demons and angels can be seen anywhere, not just when taking *ayahuasca*, because those impressions have been engraved into our neurons. Everything we have experienced is engraved in our brains — the truth and the lies, the sweet and the bitter.

Each of us has our demons, and *ayahausca* shows them to us so we can face them and heal. *Ayahuasca* teaches us the truth about ourselves. By using it, we begin to recognize who we really are. We begin to see that our pain and karma are not just ours, but also connected with our ancestors and other people.

Gradually, *ayahuasca* helps you clean out your body, and then you usually stop seeing demons. It is also helpful to clean out your body before taking *ayahuasca*. I believe that shamans undergo many purifying diets so they can see more angels and fewer demons. After the body is rid of toxins, then one begins to see the real spirits. If you follow a diet and drink a plant, you can see the spirit of the plant, and can talk to it. The spirits will take your hand and show you their world, and teach you.

Eventually, you begin to see the powerful spirits, such as the *Yacurunas*, the spirits of the water; the *Sacharunas*, the spirits of the forest; and the *Ninarunas*, the spirits of the fire. These spirits, have distinct forms and costumes that are recognizable. Runa means "man," but these spirits are not just men, but more like gods.

Sometimes I thank the people who come to my ceremonies for being willing to suffer through their visions, to struggle with their problems, and to clean up their *karma*, so that I can have fun singing and dancing and calling the spirits.

Today, I have six hundred hectares of land in the jungle where

I help people from all parts of the world. In the future I also want to work more with the children, so the tradition of using plants and natural medicines for healing is carried on by the next generation. For this reason I'm creating a children's center called "Apajonita," here in Tamshiyacu. At this center children will learn to develop different skills as well as learn about the traditions of our ancestors. I want to see positive changes in our society so that the earth is not destroyed by society's negligence.

This is a translation of an invocation which Don Agustin sings to the spirit of *ayahuasca* and *chacruna* at the beginning of the *ayahuasca* ceremonies.

We are all present here to drink ayahuasca with chacruna.
We know that ayahuasca is our medicine.
When the night is silent, then ayahuasca begins to do it's work.
When we have drunk the magic of the medicine, it is with us, and
ayahuasca and chacruna will give us visions.
From the plants that we are drinking, we now begin to have visions
and become conscious.
The magic of the medicine is working, we are all journeying,
and through our visions we are gaining knowledge of the universe.
We see the history that is within our bodies,
and finally we are healed.
All the animals, plants and spirits are happy
with what we have learned.
When dawn comes ayahuasca is in our bodies and we feel healed.

About the Author

Jaya Bear was born and raised in South Africa. After leaving there she spent many years traveling through parts of Africa, India, the Middle East, Europe and North and South America. She has lived in the United States for the past twenty-five years, and currently resides in Taos, New Mexico. An artist, entrepreneur, and organizer, she has arranged numerous workshops and large events. For more than three decades, she has worked with spiritual teachers from many traditions.

As part of her own spiritual quest she organizes journeys and workshops for people, who wish to experience deep transformative work that can bring about life changing experiences.

Jaya is the founder and director of Puma Shamanic Journeys, which currently takes small groups of people to Peru, to work with *ayahuasquero* and shaman Don Agustin Rivas Vasquez in his Amazon jungle retreat. She may be contacted at:

PUMA SHAMANIC JOURNEYS
P.O. BOX 1950
EL PRADO, N.M. 87529
USA
E-Mail: jayabear@taosnet.com
Web site: http://www.spiritjourney.net